The Publican's Handbook

Fifth Edition

Advice and ideas for running a successful pub business

The rules and regulations governing business practice in public houses and other associated topics covered in this book, including national and international legislation are subject to change. Kogan Page Limited and the editor cannot assume legal responsibility for the accuracy of any particular statement in this work. No responsibility for loss or damage occasioned to any persons acting or refraining from action as a result of the material in this publication can be accepted by the editor or publishers.

First published in 1997
This fifth edition published in 2002

Kogan Page Limited
120 Pentonville Road
London N1 9JN
www.kogan-page.co.uk

British Library Cataloguing in Publication Data

ISBN 0 7494 3846 0

Typeset by JS Typesetting, Wellingborough, Northants.
Printed and bound in Great Britain by Bell & Bain, Glasgow.

Contents

Part Three: Profitable Drinks Retailing

Keeping a safe cellar - is as easy as pulling a pint

By BOC Sureflow, the UK's leading gas supplier

As a publican, everyday you may be putting your life at risk, when protecting yourself is so easy. Carbon Dioxide (CO_2), in dispense gas, is classified as a hazardous substance. You can't see it or smell it and so you could be easily overcome by any high concentrations that could build up from gas leaks in confined areas like the cellar.

Anyone who doesn't assess the risks associated with dispense gas cylinders are unnecessarily putting themselves and their staff at risk , and could face prosecution by not complying with the Confined Spaces Regulations.

Ultimate protection from danger

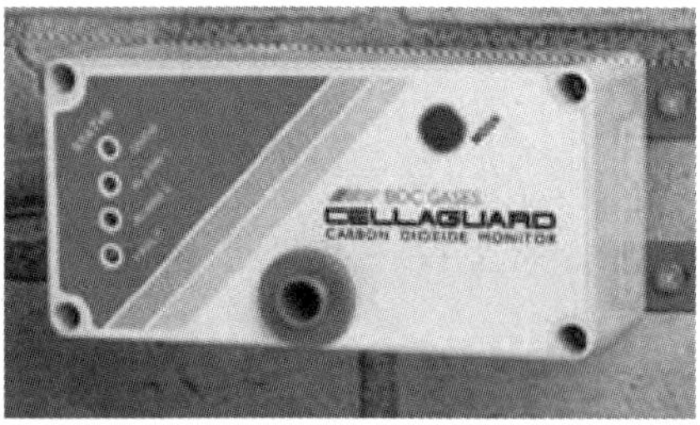

Cellaguard, is BOC Sureflow's most popular safety protection solution. This CO_2 monitor alarm will constantly test the atmosphere within the cellar. If CO_2 levels rise above set safety limits it will trigger an audible and visual alarm to warn staff not to enter the area. Even if you don't have a Cellaguard there are other ways to reduce safety hazards:

> *Over 20,000 cellars worldwide are already protected by such CO_2 monitor alarms.*

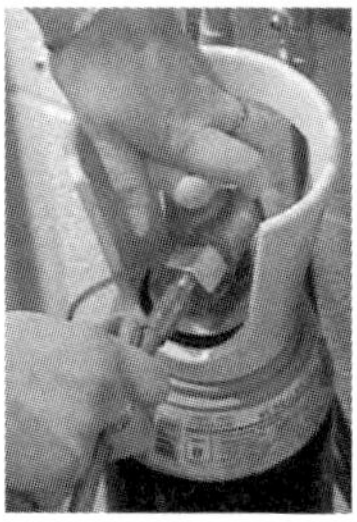

- ***Reduce the need to handle cylinders***
  Keep cylinder stocks to a minimum. Also consider installing a dispense system that minimises cylinder handling.
- ***Assess safety risks regularly***
  Risk assessment is made easy by a package from BOC to pinpoint hazards and measure the asphyxiation risks in the cellar.
- ***Train staff thoroughly***

Be CELLAWISE and stay safe

To help the industry further BOC will soon be launching a gas safety training video called CELLAWISE. This can help you to train new or existing bar staff .

At just £15 per video this "on the job" training video will demonstrate how to safely change and store cylinders and deal with (and prevent) gas leaks.

For more information

Checkout the BOC SUREFLOW Website:
www.bocsureflow.co.uk.
It is jam-packed with FREE Safety information.

Call BOC's 24-hour customer helpline on 08457 302 302

The Contributors

Martin Armitt is trade marketing manager for Douwe Egbert's Coffee Systems, responsible for marketing across a range of sectors that include pubs, hotels, restaurants, staff catering and leisure. After graduating in 1994 he went to work in a trade marketing capacity for Rothmans UK for six years prior to taking his present position. He is married with one child and lives in Buckinghamshire.

Consultant editor **Danny Blyth** is a freelance journalist specialising in licensed retailing and catering. He contributes regularly to trade titles including *PUBbusiness*, *Free House Innovations* and *Morning Advertiser* and has regular food and catering features in titles such as *Restaurant Business* and *Cost Sector Catering*. Other trade activity sees him act as a consultant on brands and publicity projects for licensed retailers and brand owners. He also writes guide books for the industry and business building features for in-house publications. Elsewhere he writes features on leisure, travel and retailing, while outside of work he cooks and gardens avidly and travels a lot, most often to Tuscany. Danny.Blythe@virgin.net

Sally Bairstow has been a journalist for over 10 years and has been writing about the pub industry since 1997 when she joined the editorial team at the *Licensee* and *Morning Advertiser*. After a 'break' working in the French Alps, she returned to the world of food and drink, first with efdex, then rejoining *Morning Advertiser* as news editor when it was bought by William Reed Publishing. The next move was to the start-up of BskyB's The Pub Channel as programme editor. In 2001, she packed up her bags and headed back to her roots to get married. She is now a freelance journalist, specialising in pubs, food and drink, living in Leicestershire and enjoying life without traffic jams on the M4 and M25. Contact: sally@bairstowgb.fsnet.co.uk

Mike Carter is the executive development chef for MasterFoodServices, foodservice division of Masterfoods (formerly Mars UK). He works with customers to tailor MasterFoodServices' wide product range to their needs, spending much of his time with publicans and pub chefs. Mike started in catering by serving an apprenticeship at the Savoy hotel. He's worked at top restaurants such as Langhans Brasserie in the West End and the Coq d'Or in Lyons. He later worked at Chef and Brewer, Baxter & Platts and Sodexho. Mike has served as a pub head chef and operations manager for a busy wine bar, so he has a very good idea of the needs and aspirations of the successful food-orientated pub. Mike is energetic, enthusiastic and passionate about food, and enjoys football and golf when the demands of his young family allow.

Patrick Dardis is business development and marketing director with Grey Archer, providers of an online ordering system and other profit-enhancing services to the pub industry. Patrick has over 21 years' experience in the pub trade. He joined Courage as a graduate trainee, then becoming trade salesman, tenanted sales manager and district manager for managed houses. After six years, he joined Whitbread as an area manager and then regional manager in the London area before moving to Guinness for six years where he helped to develop the Irish pub concept of the late 80s and early 90s. In 1996, he joined Wolverhampton & Dudley Breweries as director of pub retailing, working on the Varsity student pub brand and other concepts. His role grew as W&DB took over Marston's and Mansfield, and he played a key role in integrating these businesses and growing the company's managed estate.

Jonathan Dennys is category development manager at Bacardi-Martini Ltd. Jonathan has had extensive experience working in the category management field. Before joining Bacardi-Martini in 2001, Jonathan worked with the retail consultancy, SRCG Limited, running training sessions and facilitating category management plans with Marks & Spencer Food Division. He has also worked with Sainsbury's supermarkets during the commencement of their category management programme.

As category development manager at Bacardi-Martini, Jonathan works across both the on-trade and the off-trade. He is involved with the 'perfect serve' – educating bars on maximising profits by serving drinks in the correct way.

Ben Ellis manages the Indian Foods category for Caterplan, working on the Knorr Patak's branded range of Indian cuisine, produced specifically for the foodservice marketed in partnership with Patak's Foods Ltd. Now aged 26, Ben Ellis has worked in the kitchen and behind the bar of several local, independent pubs near his home town of Leiston, near Aldeburgh in Suffolk. Starting as dishwasher at the age of 14 he worked his way through school and then Aberystwyth University. After a year working in the US he moved back to Bristol in the UK where he studied for his Masters degree in marketing while working as a breakfast chef for

Eurest. In 1999 Ben joined Bestfoods UK Ltd. where he progressed to brand manager for Knorr, working for Caterplan – the Foodservice Division – supplying foodservice-specific products to chefs throughout the UK. In November 2000, Bestfoods and Caterplan merged with Unilever to become Unilever Bestfoods UK. He works in close contact with both the commercial and technical sides of Patak's family-owned and -run business, which he says is one of the most enjoyable aspects of his work.

Peter Farrett has been group marketing director of Brakes since January 2001. Prior to that he worked for a brewery group in a number of marketing and development roles for many years. He has much experience of both the wet and dry offerings in pubs. In the little spare time Peter has, he enjoys sports, particularly sailing.

Sue Garfitt has been director of category planning at Britvic Soft Drinks since November 2000, responsible for the management of all company pricing, promotion, range and display plans, and integrating brand and customer management. Prior to that she held positions of trading director for the on-trade and national account controller at Britvic, which she joined in January 1997.

Sue began her career with Massey Ferguson in both sales and marketing. She quickly moved on to become senior product manager at Whitworths Ltd. In 1991 she moved to Boboli (UK) where she began in a national account manager role, but was soon promoted to marketing manager with responsibility for the marketing plan and budget in the UK, Benelux and Ireland. Just prior to joining Britvic, Sue moved to Hero Drinks Group (UK) Ltd to become their trading controller and launched new flavoured water and mixer ranges.

Matthew Hudson has worked in the UK wine industry since 1982 for a number of wholesalers, most recently (since 1993) for Oddbins Corporate Business, the trade supply arm of Oddbins. He holds the Wine & Spirit Education Trust Diploma, has a keen interest in alcoholic beverages of all shapes and sizes and operates a small brewery in his back garden.

Jackie Mitchell is a seasoned food and travel writer. She trained as a journalist in the UK with IPC Magazines and Reed Business Information and worked on publications such as *Caterer & Hotelkeeper*, *Travel Weekly* and *Homes and Gardens* magazine. She then moved to Hong Kong, where she was editor of *Travelnews Asia* and PR manager of Holiday Inn Asia/Pacific, which gave her a real insight into the hospitality industry. She has also worked on magazines and newspapers in Australia and New York, USA. Her travel books include *Long Stays in Australia*.

Since her return to the UK, Jackie has written about the hospitality and catering industry for over 10 years. During that time, she has edited several publications including *European Hotelier* and *Independent Hotelier*, which won a 'Helping Hands Award' from the Federation of Small Businesses.

Jackie writes regularly for publications such as *Catering Update* and *Morning Advertiser* on the latest trends in food and drink and reports widely on food exhibitions. She writes profiles on catering operations and restaurants and interviews key players in the industry. She lives with her husband in Surrey and has two stepdaughters, who are vegetarian. Visit her website: www.jackiem.com

Elton B. Mouna is sales development manager with Fuller, Smith & Turner, based at its Griffin Brewery in Chiswick. He has risen through the ranks of the pub retailing industry following his graduation with an OND in Hotel Management and Catering Operations from Thanet Technical College. His first position was as a barman at a London pub, rising to head barman and then assistant manager before taking the first of what was to be three positions as pub manager for Fuller's at various London pubs. He won The Griffin Trophy Fuller's Pub of Year Competition whilst running The Fleetwood in the City of London. Now he has moved on to line management at the brewery and is responsible for various aspects of sales development across the Fuller's estate, including promotions and AWPs. He is married with two young sons and lives in Wapping, East London.

John McNamara joined the British Institute of Innkeeping as chief executive in January 2002. He is responsible for the BII's two arms: BII, the professional members' organisation for licensed retailers and BIIAB, the BII's wholly owned awarding body for licensed retail qualifications.

John came to the BII from the Hospitality Training Foundation where he led the two commercial divisions – Stonebow and the Hospitality Awarding Body (HAB). He has over 20 years of strategic management expertise gained within the financial sector. His appointments have included corporate director, retail area manager, business manager and training and development team leader with a major clearing bank group.

John holds graduate and post-graduate qualifications from the University of Wales, the University of Aston in Birmingham and Ashridge Management College. He is married with children.

Clive Pettitt is the marketing director of Greene King Pub Partners, the leased and tenanted division, which consists of 1080 outlets. He has been with Greene King for 28 years, and originally worked in the design of pubs before moving into the free trade and then corporate marketing. Following the acquisition of Magic, Greene King was divided into three divisions where Pettitt took on the marketing director's role of Pub Partners. Renowned in the company for moving the leased and tenanted division forward with managing director David Elliott, Pettitt and his pioneering ideas have been the catalyst for Greene King winning the Publican award, Pub Company of the Year, for the last two years.

Dominic Roskrow has been writing about the pub trade for just over 10 years. He was trained as a reporter at the *Sheffield Star*, and was entertainment reporter there until 1987, before emigrating to New Zealand, where he wrote about music for both the *NZ Herald* and the *Auckland Sun*. He joined Quantum Publishing in 1991 and among his jobs there he edited *Pub Food* and *Club Mirror*, and was features editor on *The Publican*. He became editor of *PUBbusiness* in 1999. In March 2002 he became a senior editor with John Brown Citrus Publishing, where he edits Sky Television's pub and club magazine, *The Preview*. He has written and edited several internet news services and currently contributes to Sky's Pub Channel website. He is 40 years old and is married with two young boys. domros@globalnet.co.uk

Introduction

It is high time for a bit more optimism all round in the licensed trade. A good sign of the times is that the pages of the trade press are no longer continually predicting the demise of the Great British Pub. We're all bored with that anyway – as we are about endless pessimistic tales of bootlegging and new threats from tax men, EHOs, anti-smokers et al.

There's a better story to tell. This is of an industry successfully adapting to change. Society is changing fast and perhaps no more so than in the spending of leisure time and income.

But just as the average customer no longer downs two or three pints in his lunch hour before returning early evening for a little more of the same, an increasing number of pubs are finding ever more profit from the non-traditional. Some of the best coffee to be found right now is had in pubs – also where customers get some of the best value available.

It's a similar story with soft drinks – out has gone the overpriced little pony-sized bottle of bitter lemon and in has surged upsized and profitable services of exciting new flavours of soft drinks offered in good-sized glasses with quality ice that lasts and a generous fruit garnish. Try getting that for a pub price in a hotel or restaurant!

But where the pub is really coming into its own is with food. Everything is fast improving out of sight. The quality of produce like frozen food and prepared sauces from suppliers continues to improve, allowing even those pubs with little call for catering or low levels of skill to put on something more than just acceptable. At the other end of the market an increasing number of 'gastro-pubs' are springing up to remind everybody of the opportunity that's out there with dry trade. And in places, chefs are queuing up to buy or lease pubs, lured by the chance to provide food profitably in a less formal style of operation.

It is as part of this mood of change that we introduce this revised edition of *The Publican's Handbook*, with an increased emphasis on new opportunities for growing profit.

Things are far from easy in the trade however. An increasingly demanding customer, more accustomed to high retail standards and expecting the best at all times, provides a growing challenge. The need of course is to exceed those expectations – and the key to this is better retailing.

This is the focus of this new edition. We aim to provide a series of strategies for a more innovative and professional approach to running a pub. Our series of expert contributors have written on the assumption that you already know a fair bit about the business – ours isn't a 'how to' guide for beginners. Rather they have written for competent and enterprising publicans looking for ideas on how to expand and develop their businesses.

These ideas and suggested strategies are, of course, of most use to those licensees with the 'room to manoeuvre' that comes with being either a free trader or else lessee or tenant. However, we also note that an increasing number of managers within some of the newer and smaller pub groups are allowed an element of freedom in their operations, particularly with regards to food. We trust too that we've much of interest to the manager with ambitions to get hold of a pub of their own in time.

But no matter what your publican status, we trust we have here a series of ideas that will set you on the road to better and more professional retailing.

Danny Blyth

from January to December...
Themes 2002
Peeks
CHRISTMAS CATALOGUE 2002
• Over 70 different themes available
• The UK's No1 theme decoration supplier
• Huge range of Christmas decorations • Crackers • Hats • Novelties...
...and much much MORE!
THE EVENT MAKERS
Peeks
...we are the name to remember!
t: 01202 489489
f: 01202 489400 e: info@peeks.co.uk
Reid Street, Christchurch, Dorset BH23 2BT
www.peeks.co.uk

PUB PLANTING – PAIN OR PROFIT

With many Pub Companies cutting back on planting you could be forgiven for thinking that flowers have had their day, but the truth is very different.

Planting is just as important now as ever but the styles have broadened to suit the wide range of venues now available to the public and according to a report specially prepared for the Publican magazine, 33% of potential customers decide whether to stop at a pub, on how it looks.

DIY or Contract?

If you have some knowledge and plenty of time you can achieve good results. Savings can be made if you plant your own rather than buy a complete basket from a garden centre, but you will need covered growing space if you want to put out an early display. On average baskets will need watering every day during the summer & need frequent feeding. Troughs and tubs will need partial emptying prior to planting with fresh compost & summer bedding. Checking for pests, dead heading to ensure continued flowering and general TLC will be needed throughout the summer. The results can be a real joy but unless you are dedicated it will be cheaper, when you cost your own time and the results will be better when you use a specialist contractor. A good contractor will take the hassle out of planting, producing a high standard of display, encouraging more customers through your door & leaving you free to promote other areas of your business.

Scottish & Newcastle Operations Director, Mark Hodgkinson was clear. "We use contractors such as Demita at a number of sites. Where appropriate they can provide the most effective and professional approach to both internal and external planting. They produce displays to suit the individual site and keep problems to a minimum."

So how do you choose a reputable supplier. David Scammell, M.D. of Demita believes there are only a handful of good companies operating today. "Look at who your competitors use and speak to the manager. They will give you the truth about service and reliability. Find out if their displays have won any 'In Bloom' awards. Visiting the company's web site often gives a better idea of the scope and capability of the supplier."
www.Demita.co.uk

Hand watering or watering system?

Hand watering is very time consuming and often impractical for those inaccessible planters. Again if you're dedicated the results may be better, but for the majority a micro-irrigation system will be a life saver, providing frequent watering with little trouble. However like most machines it pays to have it serviced regularly.

Damage caused from excess water dripping from the displays has caused massive refurbishment costs to pub operators over the years. David Scammell explains that this was due to poor standards of installation and not the watering systems. "Whether you hand water or use a system great attention should be paid to where the water goes. The advantage of a system is that it can deliver small amounts of water on a frequent basis, thus cutting down on wasted water. Then we make sure the water is led away from the building by for example providing our patented drip trays" (see below).

▼ Example of how not to do it

▲ Water damage

▲ Drip tray

▲ Finished display

"The Demita way"

"See before you buy" is another initiative Demita have brought to the market. Planting schemes, both new and alterations to existing can be simulated onto digital images of the site, cutting out expensive mistakes and making quotations come to life.

▲ Before

▲ Simulated

▲ Reality

To summarise, planting should only be used if it enhances your site and will draw in customers. Think carefully about the style of planting suited to your site and location. Do it yourself if you know you will put the time in to do a good job, otherwise use a professional supplier.

Once you've attracted the customer inside don't forget to consider whether interior planting will enhance the décor & atmosphere. Softening the hard edges often gives more appeal to female customers. Live or artificial plants with a great selection of pots are available. Interior & exterior displays and maintenance are available to rent or buy outright.

PLANTING FOR **PROFIT** NOT **PAIN**

Part 1

The Human Side of Business

1

Personal Dynamics

Sally Bairstow

It's about you. It's about your personality shining through. Anyone can learn to pull a pint or pour the perfect gin and tonic, but personality cannot be learnt – you're born with it – it's that whole nature vs nurture thing. You can take the publican out of the pub – but you can't take the pub out of a good publican.

I love pubs. The sheer variety of the thousands of inns and bars is incredible. What I like is that the ones you frequent regularly are familiar and the ones you've never been into before are an adventure.

What always stands out for me is not just the quality of drink, food or service but the people who work in them. They're a real mixed bag. That's the beauty of the British pub industry.

It's not just about, 'Here's your drink/food, Sir/Madam'. It's about so much more – the atmosphere, bonhomie and cheer – ABC it is, but it's certainly not as simple as this.

Textbooks and trainers will extol the virtues of a warm welcome, a smile and eye contact with your customers – but if it appears 'put on' and not completely genuine it can very easily backfire.

The beauty of the pub is it is a stage. If you think of an idea that will make you stand out from the competition – rehearse and perform. Your personality and ideas can make a difference. Be yourself, you're an invaluable resource, just as your staff are. More importantly you and your fellow workers are people – be human and not robots. It may be the service industry with the ultimate objective being to serve your customers, but many licensees will insist they are more than that – they are a friendly ear, a confidant, a shoulder to cry on and an invaluable source of local knowledge and gossip. People will come in and buy a drink just to find out the comings and goings – what a nosey bunch customers are!

It doesn't just need to be the drink that acts as a pick-me-up for customers, after all you can get that 'tonic' at home, so use your energies, dynamism and know-how to play their crucial part in the profitability of your bar.

Knowing your customers is vital. A regular can be worth thousands of pounds in your till over a year and the last thing you want to do is lose him or her to a rival down the road.

Broadly speaking the pub nearby will offer a similar range of food and drinks menus, so once again we are back to the one thing that makes *the* difference, you and your staff. As an independent publican, you can react and adapt your offering quicker than many others, so if something's not working, change it. And as the age-old adage goes, if it ain't broke, don't fix it!

Anyone who knows this industry will be the first to accept it's a hard job. Hours are long and unsociable. And anti-social is the last thing you can be in your work. You can't be there all day, every day. So, whatever you decide is the work ethos you want to portray in your bar, it must be carried through by everyone who works behind it. At the same time, everyone should be allowed to reflect their own, individual personalities.

What makes a good host? How long is that proverbial piece of string? It's horses for courses and any other analogy you'd care to throw at that question. A quick nip of a fine, single malt might loosen one's mind enough to come up with some answers! But for me it comes down to 'just being yourself'. It may sound like a load of psycho-babble (and no doubt scientists and researchers are still trying to unravel the mysteries of the human psyche) but just as in every other walk of life, you gel with some folk and not with others.

The art and craft of the good licensee, however, is not to let those ones that cause you angst bother you and to get on with the job in hand – that of mine host. That'll be how you keep the pounds and pennies falling into your till while running a public house. By its very nature, any member of the public can walk in, and you can't choose your clientele. You can encourage certain types through the service you provide, the food, drink and entertainment you lay on, and of course you always have the right to refuse to serve someone, but when hospitality is the name of the game, and you're in it to make money, it can be hard turning away someone's hard-earned cash.

Once again, it's part of the beauty of the job, the vocation. . . overcoming those trials and tribulations of the day. There aren't many jobs and industries where so many variables can affect a day's business. It's tipping it down with rain – does everyone stay at home, or go down to the pub because it is so miserable outside? These everyday challenges, which are outside your control, mean that you are always being called on to react and adapt to different situations and people all the time. Even your regulars come in in different moods; the key is to spot them. They want to chat? They want a quiet drink in the corner? Accommodate them. That is one thing in life which costs you nothing, but can make all the difference to your profits.

Be a bit quirky, take advantage of your life experiences, your character, your interests or the history of the pub or location. Fascinating facts to wow your customers will always go down a treat. The public has an inherent love of trivia; if you're a sports nut, reflect that in the events you lay on, astound drinkers with facts and figures about footie, basketball, golf or curling. . . if you're a classic car fan then deck your pub with pictures. Maybe your ancestors are Scots from the isle of Islay – make the most of your roots, specialise in Scotch and know the stories behind each and every one; it'll help sales too.

If your pub is steeped in history and maybe has its own resident ghost, find out all you can about the legend, then do your very own 'Jackanory' when customers ask about it.

The key is to be able to talk on almost every subject, have opinions, and have your own chosen specialised subject – be Mastermind! There's nothing better than a good story washed down with a great drink!

If your bar is popular with tourists, then know the history of the area, be able to recommend places of interest; you can have a captive audience and by sharing your knowledge it will make their trip all the more enjoyable.

Word of mouth and personal recommendations are the most powerful marketing tools and will keep customers coming through your doors again and again. That's where consistency of service and atmosphere is important. Set your standards and keep to them. A boss once said to me, 'If people have a good time, they'll tell their friends; if they have a bad time, they'll tell anyone and everyone who happens to listen.'

In my pub-crawling travels (since I was 18, of course, and all in the name of research!) I have popped into many a 'watering hole'. Each and every one is different, even the big branded bars – that's because there are individuals working there. It's not just the friendly efficient folk I admire, it's the characters I love.

I once met a former monk. The path he followed changed and he took on a new career ending up as the tenant of a country pub. It's little surprise he and the monastery parted company: he was renowned in the locality as terse, abrupt and verging on the downright rude. The beer wasn't even that good, but he certainly knew how to have a good craic, and that was good enough for the hundreds of customers who'd flock through his door week after week.

Another hugely popular pub was favoured by many who liked a flutter on the horses. 'Tipster Tom' certainly knew his turf and which horses and riders would be first past the finishing post. The punters, as a result, knew who to thank and where to spend their winnings.

We're all individuals, have different likes and dislikes, strengths and weaknesses. That's what makes us human, and that's what makes a pub poles apart from a vending machine. And that's what makes being a publican a never-ending challenge.

People don't go to a pub just to get a drink, so don't just serve them one. You make the difference. Make it pay and reap the rewards.

2

Tomorrow's Professional Publican

John McNamara

I would like to start this chapter with an obvious question. What's professionalism? If you think about a professional sportsman, that's someone who practises, and practises to get better and better at what they do.

I believe it was Daley Thompson who said he trained every day, including Christmas Day. 'Why Christmas Day too?' he was asked. 'Because my main rival doesn't.' A very astute response.

Today's publican is much like this. Competition is fierce – not just against other pubs, but against people's other leisure activities too. After all, many village pubs are dying out even when they are the only one left in their community. It is up to the licensee to prove to local residents why they should support the pub, why they should leave their open fires and nice warm houses to brave the elements for a drink. And if when they get there your offering is a warm glass of wine from a bottle that's been open for a week – when they could have been drinking a nice cold quality Pinot Grigio – they won't come back.

Professionalism in our sector has much in common with sport. Standards are always getting higher, the competition is getting fiercer, and licensees cannot afford to rest on their laurels. But it's the simple things that help get it right and professionalism does not mean a Daley Thompson-style training regime.

Tradition
with a
TWIST
If you want to take a closer look at what's on offer, just log onto our website and see.
With countless local pubs to let – and the chance to learn about them online – you'll be able to make a better choice about where your future belongs.
GREENE KING
17 99
FINE ALES
The Publican Awards
2002
www.greenekingpubs.co.uk

Your best assets

What are your best assets? If you don't know the answer to that question, there's a long way to go. Your best assets are you and your staff.

It is often cited in this game that it's not worth training your staff as they move on so quickly. That view's more short-sighted than the *Titanic's* navigator.

Let's look at it from the customer's point of view. They come in and order a drink. They do not say: 'I'd like to order a drink from the manager or proprietor of this establishment,' nor do they say: 'I'd like to order a drink from a full-time member of staff who has completed a training course.' What they do is order a drink from the first available member of staff – who could be the licensee or a part-time, temporary worker that started five minutes ago.

But the customer doesn't know what their position is – the quality of the service must be the same, be it from Joan or Fred who have both been with you for years, or Kylie and Lee who have been with you two minutes. To provide comprehensive staff training on or before the day they start working for you is the single most important decision a licensee can make.

This isn't just about being professional – it's about being legal. The arrival of the Criminal Justice and Police Act and the Licensing (Young Person's) Act has put the onus of responsibility for upholding the law on your staff. If they serve someone illegally, someone who is under age, or drunk, you all pay the price – server and licensee. In response to this, the BII launched the Barperson's National Certificate – a qualification that uses a self-study workbook and an assessment that is taken on the premises, over the phone, aiming to ensure that staff have a knowledge of licensing law and their responsibility in selling alcohol.

Getting and keeping those assets

Having good staff is a lovely idea – but we all know that the biggest problem is getting them in the first place, and then hanging on to them. Professionalism is going to be one of your strongest tools here.

One of the main reasons why recruitment is such a problem is the low perception of our industry. Despite the fact it now offers structured career paths backed up by a range of national qualifications, some of the fastest routes for young people to big bucks, and a flexible, sociable, fun working environment, it is not seen as a 'proper job'.

Licensees have a crucial role to play in this – not just through developing quality staff, but by acting in a socially responsible manner, and playing a part in the community, both of which we will go on to later. But in order to recruit you have to show that you want to invest in your staff and give them the pride to represent you to your customers.

And talking of customers. . .

While your staff are your best asset, your customers have a role to play too! Without them, it would be a sorry state of affairs, but customers do more than put money in the till – they should be your barometer of how well you are doing.

The one thing customers do that can help your business more than anything else is complain. A customer with a complaint, which is rectified in a more-than-satisfactory way, will be your best advert. They will tell more people how good you are than a customer who was just satisfied throughout.

Complaints procedure should be part of your very basic staff training. Customers today are far more intelligent and aware of their power. It's easy to think that complaints are going to cost you money – and we all know that customers love it when they think they have ended up with a good deal because they complained. But often complaints don't need to cost money – the customer sometimes just wants recognition that they aren't having a good time, and they want an apology. When you are running your customer complaints training, it is worth ensuring that your staff know that they should inform you when there is a problem. A personal visit and some tender loving care from 'Le Patron' works wonders.

The little things

So now your staff and customers are feeding you with information, and all know how to interact with one another, let's look at the rest of the venue.

The little things matter. A colleague's mother hated McDonald's. She thought it was a terrible idea, with terrible food. Until she went to Hong Kong. While in Hong Kong, she was told that if you want to use the loo – go to McDonald's. Now McDonald's may still offer the same food – but because its toilets were clean in Hong Kong, it's not the pariah it was.

Toilets, ashtrays, the bar, your tables – none of them take much time, but they have a hell of a negative impact if they are dirty. And the worst thing is that no one notices when they are clean.

There's nothing worse as a customer than leaning on the bar when you order your drink and coming away with wet sleeves. And then sitting down at a table covered in spilt drink, bits of crisps and with an ashtray that looks like it has been used by 50 Hungarian trade unionists. And then going to a toilet that's got no loo paper, no soap and a hand dryer with the blowing capacity of Rip Van Winkle. You get the picture – these small touches make such a difference, I cannot emphasise it enough. When you catch your bar staff clock watching, or chatting to one another as there are no customers, give them a cloth and get them cleaning and tidying. It will, without doubt, add to your profits and your image as a professional.

The bigger things

There's nothing you've read so far in this chapter that's rocket science. There's also nothing that impacts on life outside the pub – and that's what we will come on to now.

Apart from staff recruitment, the other major issue facing our industry is alcohol-related crime – especially as pubs are often seen as the problem. It is up to you to become part of the solution.

The BII, a few years ago, launched a social responsibilities initiative. This came in response to the Government's crime reduction strategy. All local authorities were asked to produce a crime and disorder audit, identifying the main problems in their area, and almost all of them identified alcohol.

Where that alcohol was being purchased or consumed (and later work conducted by the BII showed that much of it was bootlegged) was irrelevant. In fact, in some cases they just marked all the pubs on a map and claimed that those were the areas where the most offences were being committed.

As professional licensees, this is not on. As an industry we must not sell to the under-aged, or in cases of habitual drunkenness, the socially excluded. We must act in a responsible manner and work with the community. Groups such as Pubwatch and responsible retailing initiatives like 'I'll be Des', the Portman Group's drink-driving prevention programme, are worth getting involved with. It is these measures, and in these I don't apologise for including membership of the BII, that mark you out as a true professional.

Other areas along similar lines are programmes, such as Cask Marque, to reward and communicate the quality of your beer products, and the Public Places Charter on smoking, something all licensees should be signing up to, not just to avoid legislation on smoking, but to promote consumer choice and show non-smokers that we want them to be comfortable too.

Develop yourself

If you've still got any time left after training your staff, cleaning your ashtrays and forming a Pubwatch, let's think about making you as a person more professional.

It's back to training – and remember that the saying 'you can't teach an old dog new tricks' is the oldest urban myth in the book. You CAN teach an old dog new tricks, and we've got case studies to prove it.

Look at your business – you know what sells and what doesn't and what your current customers want. But do you know what's got the best gross profit margins? Do you know how to use one member of staff to motivate another? Do you know where your hot spots are? (In the pub, not on you.)

As part of its commitment to raising standards and professionalism the BII developed a suite of advanced qualifications. These tackle particular areas of the pub and have been designed to add profits to your bottom line. The range includes a certificate on wine retailing, one on leadership and motivation, and one on overall business development. I would go on, but this isn't an advert for the BII.

Don't think that there's nothing you don't know. The best operators are those that constantly innovate, constantly strive for a higher goal, and constantly look at what others are doing.

If you open your eyes, your ears and your mind – you will truly become a professional.

3

Getting the Best from Staff

Clive Pettitt

In the pub business one of the most important aspects of being successful is developing and retaining a brilliant team. Your staff will help you achieve your business objectives. By working with them in developing the business, your staff won't be the paid help, they'll become part of the success.

Changing times

Over the years we've all experienced a huge change in the industry and also continuous change in the demands of our customers. Expectations are higher, quicker service is required in this time-conscious environment, and cultural experiences with more international travel has resulted in tastes and fashions changing ever more rapidly.

With the onset of these changes, both you and your staff need to fully appreciate customers' tastes and needs to gain customers, retain them and also over-exceed their expectations. When I speak to those among our licensees whose operations stand out from the crowd, they never take all the credit for their success – as much recognition is passed on to their invaluable teams.

Team building

One outlet, the White Horse in Oakington near Cambridge won our Greene King Pub Partners Award of Excellence in Service 2001. This included winning a weekend holiday through the sponsors Holsten, but rather than go away they instead used the value of the prize to finance a party for all their staff. Their words to me were, 'We class ourselves as one big family here and by working together we've all achieved this recognition.' Gestures like this mean staff are made to feel part of the success and proud of where they work. A key component in my eyes to retaining staff is sharing the success.

There are many skills licensees require to appoint, maintain and develop good staff. The most important aspect is retaining a professional approach at all times and that means giving staff time. Remember, they want to do a good job, they just need to be shown how. By maintaining a professional approach you're not showing them whose boss – it's more of a 'follow the leader' approach.

High standards

Honesty is another key element to team building. You must be honest with them and accept and want the same honesty in return. Listen to their feedback, more often than not they've got some good ideas which can help you improve the business.

When hiring staff it's imperative that they know the culture of your outlet – exactly what you are all trying to achieve. If people know they're going to feel part of something special and proud to work there, they'll work harder to achieve and improve the high quality standards already in place.

Essential qualities

Hiring good quality staff is difficult in any business but what we always recommend to our licensees is, again, hire them professionally and you'll be halfway there. You need to find the right staff, who can work in your business, and understand and embrace the culture. Yes, they need relevant skills but the main thing is not to get too hung up on these.

You need to decide what you see as essential in a person and what's desirable. A member of staff's personality is probably more important for the continued development of the team and for the satisfaction of your customer. Skills can be taught, personality can't.

Displaying a recruitment notice outside the pub doesn't always give the best impression. You're much more likely to get a good response with a quality ad in the newspaper or actually listening to your staff and locals. Staff can often recommend someone. A person using your pub could be your next new recruit. Two positives about this: 1) they know you and 2) they like visiting your pub. This is another pointer that the owners of the aforementioned White Horse endorse; most of their staff were regulars to the pub before they employed them.

Business standards

Once you've recruited staff, we always recommend a full induction into the workplace as we do for our own Greene King personnel. Even if you've recruited someone who's got plenty of experience, it's essential they fully understand 'your' way of doing things and what both your and their expectations are. These include the conditions of employment, dress code and expected behaviour.

Irrespective of experience and skill levels, training is the key way to stay ahead of the game. A successful business has high standards and aspires continuously to be the best. To stay there, informative and relevant training is required at all levels. Even if, as a licensee, you've been in the business for years, you don't know everything. Technology, fashions and trends change and you need to keep in touch and up to date. Train yourself as well as your staff.

Review performance

To really assess training needs of your team, it's recommended that you regularly review your staff with something like a performance review. It doesn't have to be called this; other names are personal development review, training review and training needs analysis. It's a means of formally reviewing a member of staff's overall performance in the workplace and within the team. It shouldn't be the only place training and performance are discussed; if you go with the honesty theory you should be open with each other daily. However it does provide you with some time to discuss issues privately and without the regular interruptions the workplace brings.

Staff training needs not only to include upselling techniques but also to address legislation. With ongoing licensing reform and significant employment legislation changes, staff need to be kept informed and up to date.

Training matters

Training shouldn't always be provided by yourself. There are independent courses out there, eg the British Institute of Innkeepers, The Publican, GNVQs etc, but pub operators will also provide quality courses to cover all aspects of the business. At Greene King we have just introduced a five-day induction course for all licensees new to the business but the elements are such that experienced licensees or staff can attend individual days, which include merchandising, chalk boarding, marketing and finance. Trade magazines and newspapers are ideal ways to keep you and your staff up to date and provide great tips on improving the business.

Your staff could also provide and deliver training, if they communicate well and are respected in the business. Empower them to train others – it's a positive roller coaster as the staff will want to emulate them.

Another important aspect of the induction is cross-training. When staff understand each other's responsibilities they'll be all the more responsive to changes in demands and fitting into other jobs when required.

You'll always have staff that stand out from the crowd – the high achievers. It's fantastic having them around, as they motivate and inspire others to be like them. Don't, however, overburden these key staff. It's so easy to pass on everything to them when you don't thoroughly trust the standard of performance from other staff. The only way other staff will reach the same level is by being given more responsibility and responding to challenges. If you do rely too heavily on the best staff they'll become overworked and demoralised and possibly leave.

Taking ownership

By delegating to staff, they are empowered and grow as a team and as people. If they have the opportunity to look beyond their team roles they'll want to develop their skills and if you give them the chance they'll stay and do it with you. By being given real responsibility, they'll take ownership of it. Issues like standards throughout the business, sales and customer service are ideal for staff to be fully responsible for.

There's a trend to introduce incentives to improve staff performance or assist a team's output. However, it is important to understand that an incentive must be introduced to improve teamwork and the team's overall performance. It must not create a divisive culture, a 'them and us' environment.

A recent incentive introduced by one of our licensees, Ali Carter of the Ship Inn, Owlesbury, is a successful bonus scheme for kitchen staff, focused on meeting gross profit targets and keeping the kitchen clean. There are 78 tasks to keep the kitchen clean. Each week the team picks five at random from the shuffled cards numbered 1 to 78. The five areas chosen are thoroughly checked. If they score 4/5 the staff receive the bonus. Staff don't stand around doing nothing; they now clean and receive a bonus for their efforts.

What you need to remember most of all when you're reviewing your staff management is that if you've clearly set out your objectives to your team then they'll join you in getting there. If you haven't, then you'll be setting off in different directions. A smart strategy to get your business where you want it needs to include the following:

- Know your business and your aspirations.
- Know your market.
- Create a culture and communicate it effectively.
- Give staff time and room to develop and learn new skills.
- Look at personalities as well as skill levels.

- Recruit your staff relevant to your business target market.
- Train yourself and your staff.
- Make them feel part of something special.

The British Institute of Innkeeping's awarding body, BIIAB, offers a wide range of qualifications for the industry, from licence application through to career development.

These widely recognised qualifications are highly relevant and respond to the needs of pub and bar operators within today's marketplace. Whether for starters joining the industry, or for experienced personnel, there is an appropriate solution within the BIIAB qualifications portfolio. Our promise is jargon-free, practical solutions that can be applied in the workplace.

The BII is committed to making its qualifications highly accessible and delivered to excellent standards. BIIAB has over 300 approved centres through colleges, private training providers and retail companies all over the UK.

By meeting the national criteria of the Qualifications and Curriculum Authority (QCA), BIIAB qualifications have gained additional status by being part of the national framework. Qualifications in the national framework may be eligible for public funding.

As a result of QCA accreditation some of our qualifications have had a title change. This has been necessary to meet standardisation processes at QCA. The syllabus content and the assessment of these qualifications remain exactly the same as before.

A Quick Guide to What's Available

Qualifications for Licensing

Handbooks for all the qualifications for licensing are available by calling the Institute on 01276 684449 or e-mail reception @bii.org.

BIIAB Level 2 National Certificate for Licensees (NCL) (formerly National Licensee's Certificate) and Scottish Licensee's Certificate (SLC)

The NCL, available for On, Off- and Part IV licences, gives prospective licensees knowledge of basic licensing law and the social responsibilities attached to the retail sale of alcohol. It has become a virtual 'must-have' for licence applications and is widely available through BIIAB approved centres such as pub operating companies, Further & Higher Education Colleges, some universities and independent training providers.

The Scottish Licensee's Certificate (Off-Sale and all other licences) caters for the differences in law for Scotland and is accessible through BIIAB approved centres.

BIIAB Level 2 National Certificate for Door Supervisors – Licensed Premise (NCDS) (formerly Door Supervisor's National Certificate)

The NCDS provides door supervisors with the knowledge and skills required to do the job professionally. The qualification is designed in modules which can be accredited individually on the NCDS 'passport'. NCDS Stage One is a knowledge-based qualification which encompasses licensing law, health and safety regulations, arrest procedures and a variety of other topics. Stage Two includes skills training in first aid, conflict management and physical interventions. The NCDS is available through BIIAB approved centres in collaboration with City & Guilds and the Hospitality Awarding Body.

BIIAB Level 2 National Certificate for Entertainment Licensees (NCEL) (formerly Entertainment Licensee's National Certificate)

The NCEL is designed to help managers and licensees comply with a wide range of safety requirements, attain understanding of entertainment licensing law and the social responsibilities attached to running venues with a Public Entertainment Licence. The NCEL is available through BIIAB approved centres in collaboration with City & Guilds and the Hospitality Awarding Body.

Licensee's National Drugs Certificate (LNDC)

The LNDC provides licensees and managers of all types of licensed premises, from the small country pub to the inner city club venue, with an awareness of the illegal drugs scene. It provides operational guidelines to help prevent drug problems arising and also tactics to enable licensees to deal with such problems, should they arise. The LNDC is available through BIIAB approved centres in collaboration with City & Guilds and the Hospitality Awarding Body.

Qualifications for Management Induction

The Institute offers two qualifications for management induction, the Qualifying Examination Certificate (QE) and the Induction Examination Certificate (IC). Both incorporate the NCL (On) or SLC and each cover the core skills for people new to the industry. The QE and IC are widely used as induction qualifications by both managed and non-managed operators. The IC is available through BIIAB approved centres such as pub operating companies and independent training providers, while the QE is available through Further Education Colleges and independent training providers.

Qualifications for Staff Development

The Barperson's National Certificate (BNC)

The BNC is designed to equip the barperson with a clear understanding of licensing law as it applies to people working behind the bar. It delivers clear statements of the law and the responsibilities associated with serving alcoholic drinks, underage customers and dealing with difficulties. Knowledge is tested using a telephone assessment procedure and the qualification can be studied for, and taken on licensed premises.

The Professional Barperson's Qualification (PBQ)*

Intended to help licensees develop more senior staff, the PBQ is designed to develop skills to respond to a rapidly changing and competitive market environment. Delivered in-house, the qualification comprises three units:

1 Barperson's National Certificate (as above)

2 Drinks knowledge and drinks service
3 Customer service and selling skills

*available from Autumn 2002

AQ

Qualifications for Management Development

This suite of nine Advanced Qualifications (AQs) has been developed to deliver commercial benefits in specific areas. They enable licensed retailers to respond to competitive demands and to develop a highly motivated team. BIIAB approved centres have experienced staff to ensure consistently high standards of delivery. Each AQ is designed to suit managers, tenants/lessees, business development and area managers and is highly focused to encourage participants to implement ideas in the workplace.

Licensed Retail Business Development Certificate

Designed to give licensees the ability to challenge their whole business plan in the context of a competitive market and their current trade.

Licensed Retail Catering Management Certificate

Helps licensees capitalise on the growing market for good pub food by providing the knowledge to help set up and manage a pub catering operation.

Cellar & Beer Quality Management Certificate

Informs licensees how to ensure their beer is consistently served in optimum condition, to increase sales and to decrease wastage.

Customer Service Management Certificate

Gives licensees the inspiration, ideas and ability to manage excellent customer service to increase repeat business and attract new customers.

Licensed Retail Financial Management Certificate

Includes practical knowledge of basic accounting practices and terminology, enabling licensees to understand the financial structure and control of their business.

Leadership & Motivation Certificate

Enables licensees to improve staff performance and team performance through effective leadership and motivation.

Licensed Retail Practical Trainer Certificate

Shows licensees how to deliver highly practical training programmes, which fit into normal working practice and shifts, as well as producing improvements in business performance.

Spirit Retail Certificate

Designed to help licensees improve marketing, merchandising and presentation of spirits and to grow spirit sales without affecting other products.

Wine Retail Certificate

Helps licensees capitalise on the growing demand for wine in pubs, bars and restaurants and to increase sales and profit by merchandising, upselling and serving wine effectively.

Advanced Qualifications Diploma in Licensed Retailing

The AQ Diploma consolidates the different assignments completed by candidates for each of five AQ certificates into a coherent portfolio. In addition, it requires that candidates put the key components of each AQ into practice in their business and then monitor the impact that this has on the business performance. To be awarded the AQ Diploma candidates must demonstrate that they have implemented the business ideas, from the certificates they already hold, in their outlets.

For further information about the syllabuses of Institute qualifications, please contact:

Qualifications Department
The British Institute of Innkeeping
Wessex House
80 Park Street
Camberley, Surrey
GU15 3PT
Tel: 01276 684449
Fax: 01276 23045
E-mail: qualifications@bii.org
Website: www.bii.org

To apply for centre approval for your organisation, or for a current list of approved centres, please contact:

Quality Assurance Department
BIIAB
Wessex House
80 Park Street
Camberley, Surrey
GU15 3PT
Tel: 01276 684449
Fax: 01276 23045
E-mail: awards@bii.org
Website: www.bii.org

Part 2

Profitable Food Retailing

Emperor
"One-Stop Shop"
making things easy for you
We understand that you might not want to stock your bar and kitchen exclusively with Emperor products and that isn't a problem to us at all.
Why? Because by utilising our sister finance company we can help source and supply whatever equipment you choose and get you the best market rates available.
At Emperor we offer complete solutions including tailor-made products, maintenance agreements and just one point of contact regardless of which manufacturers' equipment needs attention.
We take hassle away, allowing you to concentrate on running your business!
for all your bar equipment needs
Call FREE on 0800 716582

4

Importance of Food

Danny Blyth

Income from food is the rising star of licensed retailing. Nothing else has shown so much growth over recent years – with the promise of still more to come. It isn't uncommon to meet people in the trade who are now taking over 50 per cent of their turnover from catering. Signs are that more will be joining their ranks over the next few years.

Identity crisis?

Traditionally-minded publicans have their reservations on all this. They fear for the identity of the Great British Pub and voice concerns at the loss of what was once the 'social centre' that pubs have provided to their communities.

The entry of so many chefs and sundry catering entrepreneurs into the pub trade adds to these fears, for most of those people are opportunists who have acquired an eatery at much less than the cost of a restaurant. In addition a lot of the newcomers are much less sensitive to the social traditions of the pub and its role as a community meeting place. Everyone who knows his local trade will have stories about loyal regulars suddenly turfed out after many years of supporting the local, and about darts teams disbanded and their boards ending up in skips.

Opportunity

Yet there is another side to the coin. Increasing food trade has injected some much needed funds into many a formerly ailing pub. Its growth has also added some optimism (and heaven knows there have been few reasons for that over recent years). Second, food-led operations encourage high standards, for they bring in customers expecting the restaurant experience including service and quality of food, but at much better value for money. If food quality, service, hospitality and other retailing standards – notably cleanliness – aren't fully up to scratch in a food-led pub then they're in deep trouble very quickly.

The third pleasing part of the 'pub food revolution' is that it is a sign of responsiveness. People are eating out more often, families are eating out more often too. The trade is giving customers what they want. This is particularly so in rural areas where hordes of thirsty agricultural workers have given way to customers more likely to commute to work and not prone to regular bouts of pint swilling several times a week, customers who want to relax over a good meal and some fine wine – which is their preferred idea of a good night out. I'm all for it.

All aboard?

However, just as every rural pub hasn't the trading potential to turn itself into a successful, food-led destination pub, many other houses in metropolitan and other areas aren't part of the 'revolution'. Some don't want to be, either because they don't wish it or are trading very well thank you as a wet-led venue. Others feel they haven't the skills, nor the kitchen size, nor perhaps the finance to make the change.

There are, however, things every pub can do to make more from catering. Shortage of skills or specialised staff needn't hold you back, for there is a booming market right now for both teas and coffees as there is for hand-held and snack foods of almost every variety. Plus the quality of pre-prepared foods from big suppliers in everything from frozen ready meals through to ready-to-use sauces has never been so good. Following on, help and assistance in everything from menu planning through to point-of-sale and other marketing support from these same suppliers is plentiful and generally of a very high standard.

You don't have to be a budding Gordon Ramsay to be showing more profit from food. Everyone should be on board, at least in terms of seeking out ways to increase margins.

Changing times

There is much evidence of the trade doing increasingly well. Rarely a month goes by without a big research company predicting more to be spent on eating out at pubs in the years to come. Pubs are doing a lot of things right.

Indeed a director of one of Britain's (and the world's) biggest foodservice suppliers has told me how he believes restaurants are increasingly 'rattled' by the coming of pub food – and not just by the handful with laurels from Michelin and other pundits – but by the total sector. Pub food is no longer among mothers-in-law and concupiscent Tory cabinet ministers as easy meat for TV comedians. That director's advice to the restaurant trade was, in fact, to seek ways to differentiate themselves from the rapidly improving pub sector!

Split personality

Things are far from perfect though. There seems to be a widening split in the pub food market, with gastro-pub quality (or thereabouts) on one hand and those who couldn't cook next day if their freezer and microwave were to have been nicked the night before on the other.

There's much less of the middle ground about. Remember them? Good stock in trade houses with middle-aged ladies. Not Delias but ladies too good for the school dinner service who would serve up delicious soups and stews, traditional roasts and puddings – all at superb value-for-money prices. It would appear that too many pub caterers have forgotten their own history. As customers continue to eat out more often they'll be looking for an alternative to either having to shell out big time at the gastro-house or else enjoying a simple snack service at the traditional local. The opportunity is bigger than you'd think at first. There are other opportunities too, such as local specialities; still too few pubs make a show out of local cheese, smoked fish and the like. Similar opportunities for setting your offer up as different from the rest exist with speciality food offers; there are few houses known for their great choice and quality in fish, or game, beef or cheese.

Menu for change

So the pub food phenomenon appears to have something for everyone, large kitchen or small operation, high medium or low skilled. It is with this in mind that we have much revamped our coverage of food in this year's edition. First we cover the three 'big flavours' on the nation's wish list menu – Italian, Indian and Chinese – offering advice on where and how to make more profit from them. We move on to look at the issue of catering for children and families, something that's coming to affect many pub caterers more, and winding up with some cross-sector and cross-customer group advice on adding value. We trust this new focus reflects the trade's increased determination to make more from its food offer.

5

Italian Food

Danny Blyth

For Italian read huge opportunity. Italian is widely reckoned to be the single biggest foreign food style in the UK. Think of the millions of services of pasta and pizza, sure, but add an increasing amount of services of pannini, risottos and antipasti and we get a picture of a huge and still growing market to be tapped in to.

Apart from anything else the image is *bellissimo*. Italian foods are the vanguard of the increasingly popular Mediterranean diet, which offers a dream combination of healthy eating coupled with elan. Add in TV adverts showing footballing – and flirtatious – seventy year-olds on sunny Tuscan hillsides for added appeal. There isn't a more positive image.

However it is the nature of the business opportunity that is Italian which is most exciting. There's change in the offing which amounts to better than ever scope for higher margins for the pub caterer with his eye on the ball. For while there is still an appreciable market for pubs in the old favourites like lasagne and spaghetti bolognese, today's more adventurous diner is fast developing a taste for Italian flavours and dishes to which value has been added.

Put bluntly, the traditional lasagne and chips offer at £4.95 is fast becoming eclipsed by a simpler pasta dish like linguini with porcini mushroom sauce served with shavings of parmesan which can go for up to double the typical selling price of a lasagne.

And following on from this, the really good news is that to achieve higher returns you needn't increase skill levels dramatically, nor incur greatly higher costs of ingredient.

In this heady climate there are four key means of making more from Italian food:

- adding value;
- featuring key ingredients;
- making things more interesting;
- stressing authenticity.

All four are closely linked. It's the sum of the combined parts that really makes for the 'Wow!' factor.

Make a show

Begin to add value through adding some panache to any and every service. As we are talking perceptions here even tableware can play a part. Italian dishes exude colour so show this off on quality white tableware, perhaps using outsize plates coupled with underplates.

Finishing dishes off simply and stylishly makes a great difference. Use garnishes of herbs common to Italian dishes like rosemary, oregano and basil. Make a real point of difference through the slightly unusual such as red basil.

Drizzles and spots of key flavour ingredients also add value. Balsamic vinegar makes a real impact as do flavoured olive oils such as truffle, lemon or porcini. In the same way shavings of grated parmesan set off a dish and add value. For a change try an alternative hard cheese like pecorino.

Sure, these are expensive, at times ridiculously so, but the point to remember is that you need use very little. Little drizzles make a bottle last a long time and they make a great difference to both taste and perceived value of a dish.

All such little touches certainly make dishes more interesting and appealing too. And indeed they add to the authenticity of any Italian dish, so ensure this is reflected in menu descriptions. They help especially with protein-based dishes like chicken but are tremendously effective with fish too, another food seeing increasing sales.

Add value

Meantime, you should always be on the lookout to add value to traditional favourites. Pizzas continue to prove popular, though their fast food image might restrict scope for adding value. However, adding more authentic topping ingredients like mini meat balls, spicy Italian sausage or marinated artichoke always commands a better price.

Pasta however, appears to offer much better prospects. Whereas the typical British customer of old would have felt short changed if pasta didn't come with a good dose of protein today's better travelled diner is seeking more authenticity and this means more simple dishes of pasta with sauce. We are still a long way from complete authenticity – at home most Italians would happily tuck in to a bowl of pasta with only a little butter and sage through it. However, people are increasingly prepared to pay well for an authentic dish if well presented and made from quality ingredients.

First source a good quality dried egg pasta. Point out to misguided customers who might ask how this is so and how in Italy fresh pasta is no more than a once a year wonder. For you, the caterer, a good dried egg pasta will also offer longer and better holding, plus better gripping of sauces. Add a quality sauce and serve a generous amount with perhaps a few oil drizzles, cheese or truffle shavings or porcini mushrooms.

Again, look out for new developments. Try the pasta flour and potato mixture gnocchi, or filled pastas. Today's customer is also keen to try new pasta shapes so consider some of the more unusual like mini bows or large sized ravioli.

If this 'new pasta' culture is new to you then suppliers can help, and with a lot more than just recipe ideas. People like Mediterranean specialists Ib Food will furnish you with detailed costings to show just how profitable such dishes can be – and how to use all those key flavour oils and the like most cannily. Caterplan can supply you with a complete matrix of pastas and sauces that can allow you to put on a different pasta on the menu every day for weeks. MasterFoodServices will supply you with an excellent *Out of the Pan* magazine that shows how to use its Dolmio range to capitalise on the very latest trends. There's a lot of help available out there – it's just a matter of asking.

Eyecatching

To keep your Italian offer up to date (and to keep up with the fast-learning customer) it's worthwhile adding to your stock of knowledge. For instance risottos are more and more popular these days but rare is the instance of an eye-catching example. Most pubs will use Arborio rice for this dish but many Italians will insist Arborio is really a pudding rice. There are ten major types of Italian rice, each with its own size, shape, colour and cooking properties. See Valentina Harris's excellent book *Risotto, Risotto!* for a superb guide to Italian rices and for dazzling authentic risotto recipe ideas to set yours off against the opposition.

See also the masses of regional Italian cook books that bulge the shelves at places like Waterstone's for ideas to give your offer that edge that comes from regional speciality. Such a trawl is always useful for ideas and especially with a dynamic market such as Italian food. For instance, books by Italian chef and multi-restaurateur Aldo Zilli (who is rolling out a new Italian food concept across the UK this year) will show some innovative and traditional ideas for coupling Italian flavours with that rising star in the protein world, fish.

Meantime, Italian continues to offer increased scope for upselling. Small side dishes of things like marinated herring or artichokes, or side salads heavy on the wild rocket are both totally authentic and heavily profitable. If you are looking to do the same with vegetables look to offer side dishes of marinated or grilled peppers or aubergine slices. Look to unusual colours like yellow courgette for added impact and more of the true Italian feel. You can even be eye-catching with the onion family! Use red as a rule, try red shallots or red spring onions (which Italians allow to 'bolt' over late spring/early autumn), or try cooking with ready prepared supplies of cipollini – flat, small and sweetish onions often preserved in balsamic vinegar. All this, together with a host of new lines in antipasti means that high value Italian starters are within the grasp of everyone.

Italian breads are undergoing a boom too. Ciabatta was once considered exotic, but is now common. And now we're looking at focaccia, panini and a variety of regional Italian breads too. Such a consumer appetite for things anew increases both the upselling potential of Italian as well as its scope for snack dish sales.

There's also increasing scope for Italian desserts. More and more genuine Italian ice creams and mixes are coming into foodservice and suppliers like the Italian Cake Company are constantly adding to ranges of Italian cakes and other sweet specialities.

Drinks too

Offering Italian drinks with food can also help improve sales. Italian wines are more than holding their own right now. There's an increasing interest in the juicy Barberas of Piedmont, the sweetish Marsalas of Sicily and the powerful Amarones of the North East. And all that holidaying in Tuscany is meaning that regional specialities like Vernaccia di San Gimignano are starting to appear on restaurant lists as well as quality Chiantis instead of the wicker basket plonk of old. Wines are going upmarket along with the food, and although Italian beers don't have quite the same cache, anybody with a good pizza trade is missing a real trick if they don't also offer Peroni.

Italian is mightily popular and set fair for continued growth. The real question for the pub caterer is whether to be content with lasagne and chips margins or whether to start out towards an altogether much more profitable goal.

serving suggest
Discover
Knorr
TRADEMARK REG'D
PATAK'S Original
T.M.REGD.
together
a world of
authenti
taste
ideas
menus
promotions
support
call 0800 783 3728
The KNORR culinary 'know-how' and Patak's expertise in authentic Indian food have been brought together in an exciting new range of Indian frozen cuisine.
KNORR Patak's frozen entrées are made using ONLY the best ingredients along with Patak's secret blend of herbs and spices to ensure your customers enjoy the very best in Indian authenticity.
caterplan
quality solutions for caterers
Caterplan is a trading name of Van den Bergh Foods Limited

6

Indian Food

Ben Ellis

Pubs should look to increase the quality and variety of their Indian food offering. Doing so will have a beneficial impact on your trade, footfall and bottom line. Here we look at some of the basics involved in Indian cuisine in terms of menu planning and key methods of food preparation, together with key points to bear in mind when marketing your new Indian menu.

Market background

One in four people in the UK now eat curry once a week and around half a million eat Indian food every day. More amazing still is the fact that one in every ten meals eaten out of the home is Indian in origin, so if you don't have Indian on your menu you will be missing out on a significant opportunity for increased footfall and profits.

Initially, the offering of the majority of British pubs and restaurants was limited to the ubiquitous 'chicken curry' made with curry powder, but today the market has grown to encompass a wide variety of dishes from around the exciting and varied regions of India, Pakistan and Bangladesh.

The number of Indian restaurants and takeaways in the UK has grown massively over the course of the last 10 years. There are now around 8,500 – a 50 per cent increase since 1990. The retail market for Indian has been growing year-on-year and is now worth over £500 million a year – £200 million up on 1996 inside five years!

Sadly, this market growth has not been matched within pubs, where the market for Indian has been stagnant for some time. This suggests that the Indian food offering within the UK's pubs is not yet being marketed in the right way at a local level and as a consequence, profitable business is being lost to local takeaways and restaurants.

The popularity of Indian food is roughly the same as for Italian cuisine and there are few pubs that would not offer at least one pizza or pasta dish on its core menu.

Methods of preparation

Indian food prepared from scratch and using fresh-bought ingredients can be a joy to cook. However it is very time consuming and labour intensive, and can utilise a large array of perishable raw ingredients. It also needs a fair level of skill.

To overcome these issues, while allowing you or your chef to add your own flair, consider using pre-prepared pastes. The ideal paste should be no more than ground herbs and spices, sometimes with a few extra ingredients such as ground coconut, cooked and then suspended in oil. This suspension maintains the freshness of the blends for a long period and so long as they are kept refrigerated once opened, can last for an extended period of several months. The most popular paste product within the pub sector is the Knorr Patak's range of pastes.

For a less time-consuming solution, consider using one of a range of finished sauce products, usually available to make up to 25 portions. You might well be surprised at the quality you can produce as the technology of production has come on a long way in recent years. Consider adding your own signature to the dish by adding your own fresh ingredients or garnishes such as extra chillies, garlic, fresh herbs or yoghurt. Preparation takes just minutes and any sauce you don't use can be kept chilled, usually for a few days, or even frozen.

The final solution that you could consider is to use some form of frozen entrée. Ready meals aimed specifically at the catering market have improved in quality dramatically in recent years, with many manufacturers launching ranges incorporating some very exciting regional dishes. I have recently been involved in the development of the new Knorr Patak's range of frozen Indian cuisine and was amazed at the truly authentic quality that we have been able to achieve. Most manufacturers would be only too happy to arrange a product demonstration for you through one of their sales reps and this solution could ease the pressure on your time and reduce the skill-sets required by your kitchen staff.

To make a decision on which method would best suit your pub, think carefully and realistically around issues such as the skill level of your kitchen staff (and the skill level of those covering in periods of sickness or absence), the number of dishes that you wish to add to your menu and be realistic about the number of portions that you are likely to sell per day in order to reduce costly wastage. Some basic cost and profit calculations will also be necessary.

Menu development

The next stage is to build your menu. We are currently seeing a development in consumers' tastes which have now expanded beyond the eponymous chicken tikka masala. Pioneering Indian chefs such as Meena Pathak have pushed the imagination of Britain's consumers, who are also more exposed to ethnic food due to the increase in foreign travel for business and pleasure. Bear this in mind when developing your menu – it is still true that tikka masala is by far the most popular Indian dish but to add value to your menu you could consider the addition of some more exotic and exciting dishes. If the marketing is right, your customers will be keen to experiment.

Another market trend we see coming through that is relevant to menu development is the increasing use of 'Indian' flavours in non-Indian dishes such as the tikka sandwich. Many paste or ready-to-use sauces can easily be adapted to make a delicious variety of dressings and sandwich or pie fillings.

Also bear in mind that Indian cuisine need not be limited to main-meal occasions. Given that the market for Indian cuisine is so strong, consider an Indian selection when planning a buffet lunch – pakoras, bhajis and samosas make a delicious alternative to standard pub buffets (and can be bought in frozen for convenience), especially when combined with flavoured dips such as tikka mayonnaise.

Indian food can even be extended to breakfast occasions – kedgeree, for example, is a well-loved dish that rarely features on many menus and is sure to go down well if you offer a breakfast service. By limiting yourself to a simple offering of curry with rice, you will be moving against consumer trends for lighter, spicy cuisine. Indian food does not always have to be rich or heavily sauce-based.

Marketing and promotion

Finally, we need to consider how best to bring your exciting new offering to your consumer in what is a fiercely competitive market. When on sales visits, one comment I hear above all others is how publicans would like to be able to compete with the restaurant or takeaway a few doors down from their pub. This is a tough proposition, but take advantage of the fact that many consumers will usually start or finish their evening with a drink at your bar. By tailoring your offering to them, you will be able to encourage your wet trade customers to eat in-house as well as drink.

It's also worth considering that Indian cuisine is perfectly suited to an evening involving a few drinks (the growth of Indian lagers such as Cobra or Bhangra is a testament to this) and this is another reason why a quality Indian menu or specials board could help to significantly boost your profits through increased wet sales.

Point of sale (POS) is particularly relevant when offering an Indian menu as this is not necessarily the kind of cuisine that customers will be planning to choose when visiting a local pub. Ensure your POS is both prominently displayed and suitable to your target market. 'Bum Burners Curry Club' might appeal in a noisy city-centre location, but is unlikely to go down well in a quiet country local. Many suppliers offer high quality POS, or if you want to go your own way, some will be prepared to help you with the printing of your own concept. If in doubt, the message consumers will most likely want to hear is that your Indian dishes are as authentic and as exciting as the cuisine that they would get from an Indian restaurant. A good way to do this is to highlight the history and origins of the dish on offer – for example, the region of India that the dish is from, the style of cookery used and the key ingredients of the dish.

This message also applies through every aspect of front-of-house presentation of your food offering. Most catering suppliers will be able to supply you with all the paraphernalia that you associate with a high street Indian restaurant, such as Balti dishes and condiment holders, and a small investment (usually available for under a couple of pounds a dish) will go a long way. Serve your Indian food in a Balti dish, finished with coriander, a swirl of yoghurt or maybe some grated coconut or almond slivers and you will be adding value to your menu and justifying a higher price point and GP.

Side dishes and accompaniments are also important in this respect. Minimise wastage by using frozen or long-life ambient products such as bhajis or naan breads. Poppadums are another hugely popular side dish and are easy to store, have a long shelf life and are best cooked to order in the deep fryer or microwave (pre-cooked varieties tend to be more expensive and harder to store).

In most establishments, Indian cuisine will be only one part of a varied and ever changing menu and to add value to this and really drive your proposition, consider running Indian theme days. Multi-buys, although not suited to every type of pub, are a great way to push both drink and food sales – you could approach both your wet supplier and your food wholesaler (or manufacturers' sales rep) to negotiate a deal linking beer or wine sales to Indian food. If multi-buys are not a suitable proposition to your customer base, you could pull-through more volume by extending your menu for a limited time – offer naan breads, raita (a cooling side dish made with natural yoghurt, cucumber and mint), chutneys, pickles and bhajis.

Be sure to publicise any planned event well in advance (I'd suggest taking pre-bookings) and consider allocating a proportion of your marketing budget to advertising. Again, your suppliers should be able to provide you with theme kits or recipe ideas and I am always surprised at the local interest that can be generated by such an event. It is also a great opportunity for you and your staff to have a really fun day, cooking and serving food outside of your regular menu.

Whether you tie the day to a notable date in the calendar is up to you and depends on your customer base. Some dates to consider could be Diwali – the Hindu 'Festival of Light' – which this year falls on Monday 4 November, or National Curry Week, commencing 20 October. Allow at least a couple of months to get everything in place for the promotion to run smoothly and professionally.

Indian food is one of the most popular types of cuisine in the UK, and it is also a market in rapid growth, which has yet to be seen in the independent pub sector. To see what can be achieved though, independent publicans should look to the success that has been won by some of the larger pub groups (such as JD Wetherspoon's highly popular Thursday Curry Club). With careful thought and marketing there is no reason for this concept not to work in the independent trade. Indian cookery is also a style of cuisine that can be tailored to appeal to a very large customer base and with careful thought there is much that can be done to add value and harness this great potential for growth.

7

Oriental Food

Mike Carter

Look at the shelves of your local supermarket and you can see just how popular, and what big business oriental food has become. It is now one of the fastest growing and most popular cuisines in the UK according to research organisation Mintel.

The Far Eastern sector has grown 75 per cent from 1996 to 2001 and was last year worth a staggering £348 billion. Almost 60 per cent of adults claim oriental to be their favourite cuisine.

Wider attraction

By contrast, anecdotal evidence suggests that specialist Chinese restaurants are losing popularity, as eating Far Eastern ceases to be confined to the bland Chinese takeaway. It would appear that us Brits now prefer to get our oriental fixes from our supermarkets or from the menus of our local pubs and restaurants.

What's more, the UK's acceptance of oriental cuisine has widened to take in the textures and flavours from Thailand, Singapore, Malaysia and Japan as well as classic regional Chinese dishes.

Far Eastern foods suit today's eating trends: they are quick to prepare, bright and colourful to present and healthy to eat, especially when combined with crispy stir-fried vegetables.

Few cuisines offer such colour, variety and exciting flavours. Oriental dishes are a great way of bringing excitement to your menus and added profits to your pub. They are also a great source of inspiration for your vegetarian options. And they need not be difficult or expensive to produce even for those with little or no oriental cooking experience.

Spicing up your menu can be easy even where time, money and expertise are limited. The growth in oriental cuisine has generated a myriad of pre-prepared Far Eastern products: culinary sauces, speciality rices, noodles and pastes – the range, quality and authenticity of the products on offer has increased dramatically and most wholesalers offer a good selection.

Helpful products

Do make use of culinary sauces such as Uncle Ben's Far Eastern range. They have so much to offer:

- great versatility both as finished sauces or as bases for your own creations;
- authentic flavours and textures without the need to invest in extensive new spices and ingredients;
- quick and easy to use even for those not used to Far Eastern cooking; and
- consistency, producing the same delicious results time after time.

You can use them as stir-fry bases, pour-overs, marinades and dips. Sweet and Sour, Thai Red, Black Bean, Cantonese, Spicy Szechuan, Chinese Stir Fry and Sweet Thai Chilli – the opportunities are as wide as your imagination.

Of course the classic carbohydrate accompaniment to oriental food is rice. Here too the acceptance of a variety of textures and tastes is growing, and as the perceived value of speciality rice is higher than for plain, there are added profit opportunities for the publican here as well. Look out for frozen microwaveable speciality rices. They offer rice on demand making it practical to offer oriental dishes with authentic side orders, for example, delicious Thai Coconut rice delicately scented with coconut, chives and cayenne or classic Chinese rice combining fried vegetables, eggs and mixed oriental spices. Rice brands such as Uncle Ben's have introduced single portion packs of microwaveable rices which are just great for flexibility and portion control. These products are easy to prepare, with guaranteed results, so you can afford to be a little more adventurous!

Supplier help

Approach suppliers and manufacturers for help with menu planning and recipe ideas. Companies such as my own – MasterFoodServices – have developed ranges of Far Eastern recipes specifically for pub kitchens, designed to produce delicious and attractive dishes despite the constraints of time, space, budget or oriental expertise. These are usually available via their customer help lines.

Cooking tips

Start simple by introducing just one oriental dish. Try to encourage feedback from your customers, both good and bad. If it sells, great. Then try another. If not, try to find out why – it might be because of something really simple that can be easily changed.

Stir-frying is quick – make sure you have all your ingredients prepared before starting. You may not have time for preparation once cooking. Thin strips of meat are often called for in Chinese cooking. Freeze your meat for about an hour before you cut it, just to firm it up. Preheat your wok before adding oil then let the oil get very hot before adding your ingredients. Keep ingredients moving the whole time to cook them as quickly and evenly as possible. Always cook with a long handled scoop – the heat from the wok can be fierce.

Then if you have the space and you are feeling really confident, what about a bit of oriental theatre. The speed, sizzling sounds and aroma of the wok make it ideal for front of house cooking, including cooking to order. Your customers will find it hard to resist!

Promotions and themes

If you want to promote your oriental offerings, ask suppliers for oriental posters, menus and tent cards – you might be surprised by what they can supply. Our new Spice it Up Kits are a good example.

Theme nights or menus can be great fun and a boost to business. Something different for your regular customers and a great hook for promoting your pub (posters, fliers, local press etc) to pull in some new ones.

If Far Eastern dishes prove popular with customers why not organise a theme night or offer a special themed menu to run over a week. The bright colours of the Orient plus its evocative flavours and aromas are perfect for pub promotions and easy to reproduce. We have been involved with highly successful Far Eastern promotions at all times of the year. Or you could start planning for Far Eastern fever at Chinese New Year, a two-week celebration that culminates with the Lantern festival. The exact date varies each year but will be 1 February in 2003.

Menu planning

- Create a balanced menu (not all spicy).
- Remember to offer a good range of colours, textures and flavours.
- Offer the main protein types – fish, poultry, red and white meat and don't forget a vegetarian option (there are plenty to choose from).
- Ensure that it is within kitchen capability eg equipment, time available.
- Think about added value items – like prawn crackers.
- Offer side orders for sale to complement the main course – spring rolls, crispy seaweed etc.

Deep Fried Fish with Uncle Ben's® Sweet and Sour Sauce

Black Bean and Pork Stir Fry, made with Uncle Ben's® Black Bean Culinary Sauce

- Consider the availability of ingredients.
- Consider your customers' spending power, and ensure dishes are affordable but profitable.

Creating atmosphere

- Decorate your pub with red decorations, Chinese lanterns etc. Point-of-sale suppliers such as Peakes sell plenty of attractive options.
- Offer chopsticks as an alternative to cutlery and train staff to demonstrate how to use them.
- Don't offer chocolates with coffee – add value and get in some fortune cookies.

Future trends

Oriental cuisine is here to stay and will continue its onward march into mainstream foodservice. Classic Chinese dishes are still favourite, but do keep an eye on the new emerging Far Eastern cuisines.

Thai food emerged in the UK in the 1990s; it now well established especially in London and the South-East, but you can expect it to gain ground elsewhere. Malaysian and Indonesian cuisines are also popular with consumers looking for a change from Indian and Chinese food. Vietnamese food remains less well known. Japanese is very fashionable and should appeal to the modern healthy eating customer, but be warned, its appeal tends to be upmarket and is concentrated in London and the South-East.

All in all, the growth of oriental cuisine is a great opportunity for publicans and it is here to stay.

8

Catering for Children and Families

Jackie Mitchell

British families are dining out more than ever before, which means that parents are forever searching for child-friendly venues.

Catering for families and children can be very lucrative, especially at weekends. School holidays are key times of the year, especially the long six-week summer break, as they present further opportunities to generate more family business.

The challenge is how you can make your pub more appealing to children and families. When parents walk into your pub, they want to see that children will be welcome. Getting the atmosphere right is very important to attract families and children. A smoky, dark pub full of men playing pool isn't going to appeal to them. It needs to be brightly lit with colours – bright napkins for example.

Signage saying 'Children and Families Welcome' is a good idea, with vibrant tent cards on the table. If appropriate, place a blackboard outside advertising that your pub welcomes children and families.

The family area needs to be smoke-free, while the smoking area needs to be contained and occupy a smaller area than the smoke-free one.

Some families may have driven some distance to your pub, so when they get there they want to be able to park nearby, so that it's easy for them to enter the pub with all the children's bits and pieces. Above all, remember that if you keep the kids happy, the parents will be too!

Special seating, especially high chairs for children under five, will be needed, as well as some kind of entertainment.

That's entertainment

How do you keep the kids amused? You could consider games machines or even a small area with toys. Other ideas include:

- paper tablecloths with crayons for the kids to draw pictures on: some suppliers like Brake Bros provide items such as blank pictures which the kids colour in and then put inside a cardboard tray;
- party packs or goody bags for kids filled with items like crayons and pictures for them to fill in.

If parents see these kinds of items in the pub, they will be reassured that your pub is serious about being child-friendly.

If you have a garden, you could consider some play equipment such as swings and climbing frames – even a trampoline!

Are the toilets suitable for kids? You could have a problem if the space is cramped and there are several toddlers running around. A baby-change area is also a good idea.

To promote your pub as child-friendly, you need to give that added value and understanding by actively offering services to help parents. Make it known that you can arrange to heat up baby food and that hot water is available.

Staff training is another area that needs attention. They need to have a friendly approach and enjoy working with children. The key rule here is for staff members to demonstrate as much warmth and friendliness as possible. If staff wear uniforms, make sure it's a relaxed style of dress like a polo shirt and trousers, for example. Staff also need to know about the ingredients and nutritional element of children's food in case the parents ask them about it.

Marketing the food offer

The menu is a key vehicle in marketing food to children and families. Special menus designed for kids always go down well. Suppliers like Fairway Foodservice provide 'Kids' Stuff' menus, which are based on full colour, wipe clean four-page menus, decorated with cartoons, where you can select and place up to eight stickers featuring various Fairway dishes from a choice of over 80 products.

Scholler Ice Cream has produced a 'Big Top' themed menu for kids – complete with juggling clowns, trapeze artists, knife throwers and plate spinners – which is the right size for small hands to hold. The menu features Scholler's ice cream desserts Cool Clown, Puzzles and Coupe Trio.

So here are some ideas for producing a kids' menu:

- Make it simple.
- Make it fun with cartoon characters.
- Make it small, so children can easily handle it.
- Themes are always a good idea like Scholler's 'The Big Top' or link it to a big event like the World Cup, the Jubilee or feature films like *Harry Potter* or *Monsters Inc*.

Style of service

How food is served in your pub depends very much on the type of establishment. If you have a restaurant area set aside for families, then staff can take orders and 'sell in' the food – especially desserts. If you can persuade children to order desserts, chances are the parents will join them!

Alternatively, you may prefer to run a self-service operation whereby food is ordered and paid for at the counter and delivered to numbered tables. The staff member who delivers the meal, however, can still 'sell in' desserts or other specials. It depends on what works for your particular establishment.

The food offering

What sort of food is well received by kids? The best idea is to think like a child. What did you like to eat when you were a child? If you have children, what do they like? Some kids enjoy eating the same as Mum and Dad, while others will think this is uncool. So you need to cater for both.

Keep it simple – kids need to recognise what the food is – spaghetti bolognese, for example. In the light of food scares such as BSE, some parents may ask questions about nutritional quality so you need to be prepared for that.

You may be surprised at what kids enjoy. For example, I recall one publican who ordered extra sausages thinking that a group of children would prefer sausages to lamb chops, but found the children ordered the lamb chops and the adults had the sausages.

Suppliers can give help and advice on what to offer kids. For example, McCain has produced a CD-ROM of menu ideas such as Cheesy Bean Speedsters comprising McCain Speedsters (pieces of potato in a light, crispy coating shaped as cars, trains, boats and planes), served with baked beans and a poached egg, with a sprinkle of cheese on top.

Tempt fussy appetites with food in funny shapes. Bernard Matthews offers a wide selection such as Snakes & Ladders, made of turkey meat shaped into – yes, you've guess it – a snake and a ladder, or there's Spellbinders, also made of turkey covered in a crispy crumbs in three shapes – a wizard, an owl and a thunderbolt.

Curries and ethnic meals are popular among children. These can be made up quickly using ready-made sauces like Uncle Ben's Indian Culinary sauces from MasterFoodServices.

As an alternative to chips, consider items like McCain Smiles – pieces of mashed potato formed into 'smiles'. Jacket potatoes are quick and easy to prepare and can be served with a host of different fillings such as cheese or tuna mayonnaise.

Sandwiches are a great standby for kids as they can be made quickly and easily and served throughout the day. But no matter what you offer always consider giving dishes unusual 'fun' names that will appeal to kids.

The power of the brand

Kids are more brand aware than ever before, so consider stocking branded items like M&M's vanilla dairy ice cream with mini M&Ms from Mars Confectionery. Or there's Smarties Mousse mix from Nestlé which is quick and easy to prepare, or a range of desserts from Cadbury's available through RHM Foodservice. Highlight these items on the menu and children will quickly recognise the brand names.

Vegetarianism

Vegetarianism is on the increase among children, so you need to include vegetarian options. The Vegetarian Society provides a wealth of information and recipe ideas. Quorn from Marlow Foods, a natural mushroom protein, which is high in fibre and low in fat, can be used to make dishes like Quorn Chilli or Quorn Pizza. It's available in different formats such as sausages, burgers and mince.

Food presentation tips

Use your imagination

Instead of serving ice cream in the traditional way, how about giving kids bowls of ice cream with dishes of sweets like M&Ms and Smarties and getting them to decorate their own puddings?

Don't just serve chips on their own. How about serving them with dips like mayonnaise, guacamole or tomato ketchup. Or toppings like cheese and bacon?

Vegetables can be made interesting for children, by stacking them up, making them into kebabs or stamping them into shapes.

Fish fingers are a good way to get children to eat fish. As a variation on the theme, Seafoodirect offer products like Mini Cod Crunchies and Mini Fish Nuggets.

Pizza is popular among kids as it can be handheld. Pizzas contain carbohydrates in the dough base, protein in the meat and cheese toppings, as well as vegetables. Pasta is a good standby. Younger children may enjoy HP Postman Pat Pasta Shapes from Premier International.

Keep up to date

Keep updated on the latest trends in children's food by talking to suppliers on a regular basis. They will have their finger on the pulse. Visiting supermarkets is also a good idea to see the latest developments in food offerings for children, as the line between retailing and catering products becomes more blurred. Keep an eye on the media for the latest film releases and kids' crazes. *Harry Potter*, *Lord of the Rings* and *Monsters Inc*. all offer opportunities for theming menus and food.

Marketing tips

- Offer kids' meal deals – a small meal and a soft drink at a set price – or 'two for the price of one' – two kids' meals for the price of one.
- Put point of sale material at kids' eye level in the family area.
- Keeping kids amused is the key to success – stock activity packs and crayons and run kids' clubs.
- Serve draught soft drinks for kids in branded paper cups.
- Hold theme days – Italian, Indian, Chinese and decorate the pub accordingly. Give the kids hats to wear or special goody bags.
- Advertise in the local paper that your pub welcomes children and families, although 'word of mouth' works wonders.

Help with marketing is also available from a wider range of suppliers. Many are offering much more than just a recipe advice service these days. Look at the list of catering suppliers on page 52 and find out what each has to offer.

9

Upselling and Adding Value

Peter Farrett

Pub food is big business. I don't have to tell you that. Around 40 per cent of all leisure time meals eaten out of the home are pub food so there are a lot of people out there looking for somewhere to eat. Somewhere they consider good enough to go back to. Somewhere like your pub? It's up to you to make certain it is. And to make sure they know where you are and how to get there.

Once you have got them there, of course, you have to make the most of every selling opportunity you have, particularly when it comes to your food offering, always remembering that if your customers don't enjoy the total experience, they won't come back.

Be different

Casual dining is on the increase. It is estimated that approximately 21 per cent of people eat out at least once a month. They want to eat healthily without indulging, except for that special occasion. Your menu should reflect that. Current research shows that people are opting for starters rather than desserts. Check that your menu offers a better choice than your local competition.

Upsell

Staff are key to upselling. All customers like to feel wanted and there is no surer way to upset them than by hard sell. Train your staff to be subtle, to offer extras in such a way that the customer thinks it is their idea rather than your opportunity for more business. Bonus your staff on selling extras so they actually want to do it. That way it will become part of their natural technique and will be much more effective.

Your menus should be easily accessible. Have them on the bar so customers can see them as soon as they walk in. That way even people who just come in for a drink might be tempted.

Have a range of nibbles and starter items that can be offered while customers are drinking and looking at the menu. That will get their taste buds tingling and make them much more receptive to what they are reading. Offering items separately on your menu gives more opportunity for adding extras to an order.

Make sure there are complementary items to go with the main meals and ensure your staff know enough about them to sell the benefits. Don't just offer steak, have a range of sauces. You're bound to have curries on your menu as they are very popular – and so are the extras that go with them. And they are very easy to obtain from your usual food suppliers these days.

The days of a wilted salad garnish on a hot plate should be well and truly over. Offer salads and vegetables as side dishes. There is much publicity in the consumer press about eating five portions of fruit and vegetables a day. This is one way for your customers to feel they are eating a healthy diet and an ideal opportunity for upselling on your part!

Give your dishes interesting names to entice customers to try them. It's an easy way to add value to a meal. And don't forget coffee can be very profitable. Have a good range on hand for people to choose from. That will also give an opportunity for selling liqueurs.

Presentation

Presentation is most important when it comes to encouraging visitors and enticing them back. And presentation means the whole experience – from the first thing they see when they approach your premises to your parting words as they leave. The food offering is just part of this experience, albeit an integral one. When you are giving thought to your menu items, think about how they will look on the plate. Is your crockery up to date? Does it make the food look inviting? There are plenty of new styles around that could give your food a lift. Keep your eye on the catering magazines – they are always good indicators of what is in fashion.

Your style is important and says a lot about who you are trying to attract and what you have to offer. This same sense of style should filter through your food presentation. This will be vastly different if you are trying to attract families rather than the grey market and should be instantly recognisable when people are searching for somewhere to eat.

Targeting the customer

Of course you can only set your style once you know who you are targeting. If yours is a pub that has a number of customers who come more for a drink than to eat, then make sure you have an extensive bar snack menu. If your customers don't have time to sit down for a meal, offer quick service at the bar and somewhere comfortable and convenient to eat. Older customers usually have more time so you can provide more leisurely eating facilities, although pricing could be more of a factor to be taken into account here.

Once you have decided who you want to attract, you need to set the offer accordingly. And the best way of finding out what your customers want is to ask them. Question them on where else they have been to eat and what they enjoyed about it. Why not invite some customers to a more formal session on a quiet night during the week. Lay on some drink and nibbles and keep the conversation flowing around what they look for when they visit a pub. It's another way of making your customers feel wanted and you could get some useful information out of it. Of course, you do have to make a commitment to make changes should they appear necessary. There is no point in asking questions otherwise.

You should always be up to date with what your competitors are doing. If they are busy, then they are obviously doing something right and you need to be in the know. If you are busier than they are, try to analyse why and capitalise on it.

All this will go towards adding value for your customers, and profits for yourselves.

Service

Service is all important. It can make or break the dining out experience and be the crucial difference you can offer over the competition. In addition to the usual attributes of being friendly and helpful, staff should also be knowledgeable about the food you have on offer. They should be familiar with all the items on your menu and be able to inform customers of the right choices. This should include knowing about ingredients – don't forget it is necessary for them to know your policy on genetically modified ingredients, and they should also be able to advise on other ingredients for customers with allergies or special diets. Having special meals readily available (frozen food manufacturers like Brakes will have excellent standbys) gives you an extra point of difference for when such needs arise.

Staff training is vital. They should enjoy their work and want to serve their customers. Again style is important. If you are a gastro-pub, you don't want serving staff with lots of kids' badges. Equally, if your client base is mainly families, having the right staff can make the difference between happy children and chaotic service!

Speed of service is another factor that must be watched carefully. Lunchtime trade usually needs to be quicker than the evening as people have less time. Quicker service means people will eat with their drink if they know they can stick to their timetable. Giving your staff an electronic order pad utilising new technology means drinks orders can be placed quickly and automatically while food orders are being chewed over.

Other areas of technology are useful too. Your own website is a must. People browse the web more and more when finding somewhere new to go. Keep it up to date and make it interesting. If people are intrigued or excited by your offering they are more likely to follow it up.

Why not establish a customer loyalty scheme? Offering a free meal or bottle of wine for regular visits is an easy way of ensuring repeat custom and also allows you to build a database of customers. This gives you an ideal opportunity to send out promotional offers and news of theme nights, special deals, etc. Ideally, write to your customers at least five or six times a year with a short newsletter.

A birthday club is another way of encouraging repeat trade. Send your registered customers a congratulatory letter or card together with the offer of a reduced price meal. It's one way of ensuring they spend the celebration with you.

Keep up with trends

To keep your food offering and your presentation up to date, you must visit as many of your competitors as you can – and not just in your local area. People will travel if they know they are going to have a good experience. Check out cutting-edge restaurants in other parts of the country. Trade magazines will keep you up to date on who is hot and who is not.

Retail trends also have a distinct bearing on what happens in out-of-home eating. Just checking out the cabinets in your local supermarket or watching the adverts on television will let you know what food trends are emerging. And with hundreds of columns of food information being printed in newspapers and magazines each week there really is no reason not to be kept fully informed.

Again, ask your customers; they will act as a good barometer for you.

Top tips for adding value

- Know your customers and target accordingly.
- Keep up to date with trends.
- Ensure your food offering matches your chosen style of customer.
- Train your staff to give first class service.
- Make your pub a destination outlet so people want to keep coming back for more.

FOOD AND CATERING SUPPLIER CONTACTS

Food and catering suppliers today offer a wide range of help and support services to the pub caterer. There's a lot more on offer apart from how to use their products and recipe ideas to help you avoid menu fatigue, such as:

- free product samples;
- advice on adding value and improving GP;
- free subscriptions to newsletters;
- catering advisory services;
- tips on merchandising and selling;
- free point-of-sale material;
- buyers' clubs and discount schemes;
- research information for the caterer;
- advice on making the most of market trends.

There's so very much out there for the asking. Try the following companies:

Aberna 01256 744500, www.aberna.com
AFE Online 0116 281 6000
Alaska Salmon 020 8607 0349, www.alaskaseafood.org
Apetito Group 01225 753636, www.apetito.com
Authentic Food Co. 0161 480 8651, www.theauthenticfoodcompany.co.uk
Aviko 01442 879933, www.aviko.nl
Beanies Health Foods 01489 574593, info@beanieshealthfoods.co.uk
F.Bender 020 8829 2302
Bernard Matthews Foodservice 01603 872611
Bonnet Cidelcem Limited 01494 464470, www.bonnetcidelcem.com
Brake Bros. 0845 6069090, www.brake.co.uk
Brambles 01642 230316
Bread Roll Co. 01727 818000
British Potato Council 01865 782276, www.potato.org.uk
British Poussin 01606 892989
British Trout Association 020 7935 5404, www.britishtrout.co.uk
Caravell 01280 826600, www.caravell.co.uk
Caterplan (Knorr Patak) 0800 783 3728, www.caterplan.co.uk
Cherry Valley 01472-371271, www.cherryvalley.co.uk
Churchill 01782 524352
Coffee Classics/FryersAzkoyen 01327 300744
G.Costa 01622 713300, www.bluedragon.com
Daloon 01636 701000, sales@daloonuk.com
Deli France 0116 257 1871, www.delifrance.com

Discovery Foods 0800 018 0002, www.discoveryfoods.co.uk
Douwe Egberts 020 8236 5015, www.douweegberts.com
Duni 01928 712377
Dudson 01782 819337
Electrolux 0121 220 2800, www.electrolux.co.uk
Enodis 0114 257 0100, www.enodis.com
Equip Line 01895 272236
Fagor 01732 860360, www.fagorindustrial.com
Falcon Foodservice Equipment 01324 554221
Fairway Foodservice, tel: 01422 319100; www.fairwayfoodservice.com
Farm Frites 01452 415845, www.farmfrites.com
Findus 0800 2854 6279, www.findusfoodservices.co.uk
First Choice Coffee 01582 418222
Fort James 0114 285 6666
Foster 0500 691122, www.fosterrefrigerator.co.uk
Frialator 01925 821280
Fridays 01580 710223, sales@Fridays.co.uk
Funnybones 01923 251224
Gram UK 01322 616900, www.gram/commercial.com
Grampian Foodservice 01953 457 719, www.gcfg.com
Green Label 01473 735456, www.greenlabel.co.uk
Grey Archer 0845 603 1188, www.greyarcher.com
RH Hall 01442 875578
Hobart 07002 101101, www.hobartmfg.co.uk
Honeytop Speciality Foods 01582 671611, www.honeytop.co.uk
iB Food 0800 252522, www.ibfood.com
Interlevin 01332 850090, tradesales@interlevin.co.uk
Kraft 01242 236101
Lamb Weston 01489 565826, www.lambweston.com
Larderfresh 0845 606 9090
Lord Chips 01233 206000
Macphie 01569 740621, www.macphie.co.uk
M&J Seafoods 01296 588260, www.mjseafoods.co.uk
Maggi Helpline on 0800 742842
Marlow Foods, Quorn Catering Information Service 0870 607 0182
MasterFoodServices 0800-952 0011, thechef.mfs@masterfoodservices.com
Matthew Walker 01773 760121
McCain 01723 584141
Nescafé 020 8686 3333
Nichols Foods 01924 272900
Norwegian Seafoods Export Council 0800 028 7175
Porkka 01923 779929, www.porkka.co.uk
Premier International, tel: 01223 233333; www.premierbrands.com
Pritchitt's 020 8290 7000, www.pritchitt.com

Rational UK 0800 3892944
Redwood 01506 400557, www.redwoodfoods.co.uk
Rombouts 01753 801299
Royal Doulton 01782 404180, www.royal-doulton.com
Royal Greenland 0161 485 8385, www.royalgreenland.com
Samsung (Apuro) 0121 744 0968
Sandwich Supplies 01633 833500, www.sandwich-supplies.co.uk
Sarah Lee Foodservice 01904 687100
Scholler Ice Cream 01483 205500
Sharwood's 0800 3284246, www.rhmfoodservice.co.uk
Sea Fish Industry Authority 0131 558 3331, www.seafish.co.uk
Seafoodirect, tel: 08000 851549; www.seafoodirect.co.uk
Silver Spoon 01733 563171
Steelite International 01782 821000
Tetley Foodservice 020 8575 5506
3663 Advice Line 08701 3663 000, advice_centre@3663.co.uk
Tilda 01708 717666, www.tilda.com
Trauffler, 020 7251 0240, www.trauffler.com
True Refrigeration 0800 783 8783, www.truemfg.com
Tryton Foodservice 01482 223223
Universe Foodservice 01932 838020, foodservice@universe-foods.co.uk
Vandermoortele 020 8577 2727
Vegetarian Society 0161 925 2000, www.vegsoc.org
Veetee 01634 290092, www.vetee.com
Victor 01274 722125
Villeroy & Boch, 020 8871 0011, www.villeroy-boch.co.uk
Wedgwood Hotelware 01782 282319
Westler Foods 01653 693966, www.westlerfoods.com
Westmill Foods 01279 658473, www.westmill-foodservice.com
Williams 0800 526517, www.williams-refrigeration.co.uk

Part 3

Profitable Drinks Retailing

10

Coffee Sales

Martin Armitt

Some good news: as a sector, Britain's pubs are doing well out of coffee. Pubs sell on average 20,000 cups a year – 17 per cent of sales outside of the home (expected to top 20 per cent in the next two to three years). The pub sector is now ahead of sales in sectors like quick service restaurants and even hotels.

Cash profit

The challenge for the go-ahead independent licensee now is to increase profit. I suggest that the first step here means a change in thinking. It means a change away from concentrating on the cost and percentage margin and toward cash margins.

A lot of licensees are at present sourcing coffee at 5 to 10 pence a cup, on which they're making 80 to 90 per cent margins. Fine enough, but the longer you concentrate on low priced sourcing the further you'll travel down the low quality route. What I recommend is moving more towards roast or ground coffee or to espresso (if you aren't already there). Of course, higher quality means higher purchase cost and lower percentage margin – but it will also yield a greater cash margin.

Quality counts

Every consumer maintains quality standard and expected price subconsciously. By moving from the quality associated with the 70p–90p cup to the £1.20–£1.30 cup you'll be meeting customer expectations. And signs from the retail sector suggest that people are indeed looking to 'trade up'.

Take the supermarkets, perhaps the most 'democratic' expression of trends. Here, people who had been buying the old fashioned instant granule products have moved on the premium versions such as Gold Blend and Douwe Egbert's own Continental Gold. Those who have previously been taking these premium products have traded up to roast and ground products, and previous customers for these have moved on to start taking more of the espresso type coffees at the highest price point.

The lesson is clear. Despite home consumption being an everyday affair and not a treat, people are becoming used to a better quality. And when they venture into licensed premises they will expect to be offered at least as good a quality – and perhaps a treat.

Top tips

I therefore recommend a three point approach to exceeding the expectations of today's more demanding consumer:

Quality

Concentrate on the quality of product. Source a quality that, while it might be a little dearer to source, will appeal to today's more 'faddy' customer.

Water quality

Water quality is often ignored. Strange when you consider that water forms an average 98 per cent of any cup of coffee. Large parts of the country are hard water areas, places where a water filter or softener really is needed. At Douwe Egbert we take this quality issue so seriously we supply a water filter where it is required free of charge.

Quality delivery

Remove the problem of deteriorating quality by removing the pour over machine. Apart from the wastage problem, pour overs also mean that a good brew is often left for too long. After 30 minutes coffee oxidises and rapidly loses flavour and aroma. Consider joining the growing number of pubs that employ systems which brew cups individually, like our own push-button Cafitesse system. Such systems improve quality in the cup by delivering fresh and aromatic brew while also cutting out waste and pilfering.

Compete wider

Once you have sourced a better quality product (be it roasted ground, or espresso type) and the means to deliver it (be it push button system or barrista) you are on a much better footing to take on the high street coffee chains at their own game.

This is worthwhile, for coffee is very profitable and after all, today's pub is becoming just as much to do with catering as it is boozing. And right now, very few high street coffee names are making money, whereas you with your pub have an altogether more 'rounded business' with the ability to make a much more varied and superior catering offer. Good coffee should be part of this.

Time counts

Timing is important in making the most from coffee. Statistics show that two thirds of all coffee drunk in the UK is consumed before 1 pm. For the pub opening at 11 am that only leaves a two-hour window for peak sales.

What's needed is to attract in more shoppers, tourists and the like in the afternoons. And first, people have got to be persuaded that your pub seems, quite simply, a nice place to stop for a coffee. A frontage that allows a sight into the interior helps a lot, especially if coupled with an open door and a view inside that shows a pub that is clean, bright and 'airy'. Second, there needs to be a strong visibility, the coffee machine needs to be in sight – customers must know coffee can be had and is on sale now. Perhaps you could use an A-board outside.

What you should certainly do is use quality point-of-sale materials, both externally and internally. This certainly helps awareness, especially if that POS is branded by a well-known supplier. Branding does work – just recently I've witnessed how a big high street store we supply has increased sales by 15 per cent as a direct result of branding by a name customers know and respect. The same works just as well for pubs. Branding reassures customers of both quality and value for money.

Look to combine branded POS with coffee menus, showing the choice of what you have to offer, together with any afternoon promotions. Also list any pastries, biscuits or snack service you have available to encourage further sales. A bright and airy pub doing a good afternoon coffee trade will even come to smell of the product and this will in turn attract trade – in many ways the exact inverse of the effect from last night's beer!

Size matters

Also, be aware of trends on sizing. Signs are strong that consumers are looking for a greater volume in a service. Today's average serving of 7oz is fast turning into at least 9oz. One major petrol retailer we supply is now even moving from a 12oz to a 20oz serving. There are several things you can do here to keep abreast.

First you could simply change from cup and saucer to mugs. Not everyday mugs mind you, but stylish long mugs that can be heavy to lift and which encourage customers to 'feel the weight'. Feeling bold? Try takeaway cups, but nice quality, branded takeaway cups. Many people feel very comfortable with them and their quality has really improved over recent years. Or, if you have an espresso or barrista operation and there's disquiet over portion size you could offer and promote Café Americano, Latte or Cappuccino. Whatever you do, effect your changes so that any upsizing also means a higher cash margin, regardless of percentages.

Reading the grains

Looking to the future the first thing to realise is that the market will not be returning to economy products. And so the onus is on pubs to improve their offer and that means moving towards roast or ground, possibly espresso.

Sizes will increase so if you are to change your offer, bear this in mind while choosing new crockery. And we'll continue to drink more milk – right now Britain is the oddball in Europe as it drinks more milk than coffee, so ensure you have milky coffees in your offer.

Don't, however, invest much in decaffeinated. Over 90 per cent of coffee sales remain for regular caffinated coffee. It is best to keep a small supply in instant sachets rather than risk costly wastage from a product prone to slow and low turnover.

Finally, if the trade is allowed wider possible trading hours expect a growing opportunity for coffee sales, particularly if you open earlier in the mornings so as to catch the all important 'coffee rush hour' that peaks about 9 am. And as the trade comes to rely more on food business, those pubs that make more of an effort to link coffee sales with desserts (and possibly also liqueurs and aperitifs) can also look forward to improved turnover from coffee sales.

From almost nowhere a generation ago, coffee is now a profitable and growing part of the average pub's business. The quality-focused above-average pub really can make some money from this drink.

11

Soft Drinks Sales

Sue Garfitt

Soft drinks are now the third largest category in the on-trade, appealing to an ever-widening range of pub-goers who are demanding choice, variety and value when going out for a drink.

Last year, sales of soft drinks in total brewers outlets stood at £1.8 billion,[1] making soft drinks more important than cider, wine, flavoured alcoholic beverages and champagne.

To make this profit opportunity even larger this year, it is vital that you understand the importance of soft drinks in your customers' lives and realise that soft drinks can be very profitable if you stock the right products and merchandise them correctly.

Pubs are pleasure destinations where people go primarily to eat, drink or participate in an activity – and soft drinks play an important part in the overall experience. Our own Right Choice category management programme is helping publicans across the board to offer the right soft drinks for these occasions in order to keep their customers happy and secure return visits.

At Britvic we are continuously researching the market and innovating accordingly to provide the right brands with the right marketing support, as well as offering licensees the benefits of our latest research. Right Choice has identified four key areas to deliver on-trade growth – females, kids, meals, and variety and value. We have developed these strategies together with a range of occasions to help grow the overall sales and profits from soft drinks.

Variety and value

Offering your customers variety and value for a full range of drinking occasions is vital – whether your outlet serves as 'the regular', an 'in meeting place' or somewhere to chat over a drink or to enjoy a meal, with or without the kids.

Soft drinks are a positive choice in their own right. However, adults' soft drink tastes are plainly different from kids' and outlets need to move beyond solely offering fizzy drinks on tap if they are to make healthy profits from soft drinks.

Whilst draught drinks are still core to the on-trade, packaged soft drinks are becoming increasingly important and can bring you extra revenue. Many pub customers are unaware of the choice available in premium-packaged drinks and are automatically served draught cola, lemonade or orange. Providing a broad range which offers a balance between draught and packaged products will satisfy more of your customers more often. Whereas premium packaged drinks account for 38 per cent of soft drinks volumes, they make up 48 per cent of soft drinks value.[1] When asked, 6 out of 10 customers said they would prefer packaged to draught[2] as they want to enjoy their favourite drink in perfect condition and are willing to pay more for it.

Cola accounts for almost half of on-trade soft drinks sales and to take full advantage of this important sub-category and satisfy consumer demand for quality, offer cola in glass bottles, like Pepsi's new 300ml, as well as upsizing draught servings to 16oz glasses.

Adults' soft drinks choices are evolving and they want offerings that match not only on-trade occasions but also their lifestyle choices. Still drinks are increasingly popular as consumers become more health-conscious and now account for almost 50 per cent of soft drinks sales in the total market. Juices are no longer demanded solely as mixers but as a drink on their own, and your range should reflect this, offering longer-serve premium juices and juice drinks to keep drinkers in the round. In the on-trade, J_2O, the premium-packaged, still, 50 per cent juice drink, was the star performer of last year, growing 80 per cent in value and 77 per cent in volume.[2]

Hot tips

- Ask customers if they would like a premium packaged soft drink – one in three will upsize if prompted.
- Clearly communicate special promotions.
- Name your smallest draught serving 'kids' to encourage adults to trade up.
- Always serve soft drinks chilled.
- Display single serve soft drinks such as J_2O behind the bar.

---

[1] AC Nielsen MAT Dec 2001

[2] USA Crest 1998

Females

Catering for women is becoming increasingly important as they now account for 61 per cent of adult soft drink consumption in the on-trade.[3] Whether it's a quick drink after work, a quiet drink with friends, a family day trip or a big night out, women clientele will have their own specific demands and they are typically more adventurous and more health aware in their soft drink choices. (I know I am!)

Soft drinks need to be more than simply for quenching thirst. If the right brands are available, people buy them as a positive choice because it makes them look and feel good. Make sure your soft drinks offering includes something a bit special beyond your standard fizzy range, such as Amé.

Hot tips

- Ensure your customers are aware of your soft drinks range by using display and point of sale.
- Offer special promotions and off-peak pricing.
- Keep chillers well-stocked and visible.

Meals

The pub food market is continuing its steady growth and is forecast to be worth £7.2 billion by 2004.[4] Because nearly half of pub diners order a soft drink to accompany their meal, soft drinks are hugely important to this occasion. Make sure you have a wide range on offer to suit your clientele, be it adults enjoying a formal meal, a quick snack or lunch out with the kids.

Hot tips

- Encourage staff to always ask customers if they would like a drink when they place a food order.
- Communicate your soft drinks offering as part of the menu.
- Offer special meal deals which include soft drinks.

Family

The family pub environment is becoming increasingly popular, with a third of all pub visits now involving children. Your outlet may cater for family meals at weekends or even be a family destination, where consumers are willing to travel a considerable distance at weekends, school holidays and early evenings to indulge their children in a big way with activities, food and drink that are very kids-focused.

---

[3] PAS June 1999

[4] Whitbread

You should cater for kids by offering both draught and specific kids packaged serves. Satisfied kids mean satisfied parents and outlets that offer the right brands and the right facilities can look forward to big profits. The pub is a real treat for kids, with almost half allowed to choose their own soft drink.

Image is very important to kids, who have high brand awareness, and they will want the perfect serve – a drink that is credible, looks right, tastes right and provides the right amount of refreshment. Premium brands and widely advertised ranges are children's top choices and also top of the league for profitability. Sports packs, like Fruit Shoot from Robinsons, are increasingly popular and mums like them too as they are non-spill.

Hot tips

- Ensure your range includes both fizzy and still drinks.
- Stock brands that your young customers recognise and want.
- Use special kids branded menus and activities.

Merchandising and back bar

As the range of soft drinks increases, there is now a great deal of choice available to pub visitors. Good range management and display are therefore essential in order for them to be aware of this extensive choice and therefore potentially buy more on each visit.

We always recommend you display and serve premium-packaged soft drinks from the chiller, concentrating on the more impulse products like J_2O. To assist selection, plan your chiller layout in a logical manner. Group brands in blocks and stack in rows vertically to grab attention and ensure that labels always face outwards.

To make drinkers aware of the full range, we also advise that pubs display the range of soft drinks on offer on the back bar, utilising a back bar display unit where possible. However, never sell from bottle displays – use these for maximum display effect only and sell the displayed brands chilled from the fridge. People will switch brands if their first choice is not chilled.

In addition, support major brands with 'at table' point of sale so that people who do not go to the bar are aware of the soft drinks available. When serving soft drinks, always offer a glass with ice and a wedge of fruit to give the very best presentation to your customers and ensure they come back for more.

At Britvic, we have developed a number of strategies and tactics to help licensees identify the 'occasions' that take place in their outlet and therefore ensure they have the most appropriate soft drinks range, promotions, pricing and display to ensure maximum returns from this important part of their total offer.

12

Improving Wine Profitability

Matthew Hudson

They say of wine merchants that if you put three of us in a room together you'll end up with four opinions, but one thing upon which we all agree is the astonishing change there has been in the wine trade over the past 20 years.

The New World has emerged in the wines of Australasia and South America; and post-apartheid South Africa is showing a dazzling variety of serious wines. Back in the 'Old World', winemakers who had been rather blasé about standards have had to look to their laurels in order to compete. Quality from the classic regions of Europe has arguably never been higher.

Profit opportunity

At the start of the 80s the UK was a reticent consumer of wine, but since then – while the UK is not drinking much more alcohol – the volume of wine drunk has increased threefold to over 17 litres per capita per year. Wine has become demystified. This offers the publican an excellent profit opportunity.

That opportunity is set to improve too, for by European standards, the UK consumer is still underdeveloped (your average Italian, lucky fellow, drinks 50 litres a year). Experts reckon that wine drinking in the UK will rise faster than any other country over the next five years.

House choice

But as consumers become more educated and confident with wine the enterprising on-trader has increasingly upped the ante by demanding a better quality of product, particularly at the key 'house wine' end of the list. So the dodgy vin de table has been supplanted by decent vin de pays or better.

Similarly, the improvements in quality of pub wine have been well documented recently. A publican of my acquaintance baulked at the prospect of losing his 10-litre boxes: 'But I can sell wine from the box at £1.60 a glass – to make the same margin on this wine I'll have to put it out at £2.20 – and my customers won't like it!'

A remarkable thing happened – although he was right that the customers did grumble, he actually sold twice as much wine! Customers came back for a second glass of this decent wine where they never did with boxed. (See the cartoon on page 70). Twice the till ring, twice a higher cash margin and more pleasure for the (albeit slightly poorer) customer.

Self questioning

Any publican wanting to improve the wine sales should as a general rule be asking themselves the following key question:

- Does the quality of my house wine adequately reflect the standards and aspirations of my establishment – and those of my customers?

This governs the approach to a product likely to account for 60 per cent or more of one's wine sales. It involves decisions – taken hand-in-hand with one's supplier or suppliers – like whether one chooses for the long-term or whether one uses a revolving selection like a 'House Wine of the Month'. Perhaps most importantly there is the cost and selling price of the wine.

Pricing matters

Consider the following breakdown of the cost components of a wine (EU produced) costing £3.00 a bottle inc. VAT (£30.64p per dozen ex VAT):

- *Duty £1.16p*
- *VAT 45p*
- *Margin to supplier 60p*
- *Packing, freight etc. 25p*
- *Oh, nearly forgot – the wine itself 54p*
- *Total £3.00*

Think about your own margin: if you work on 65 per cent you are going to end up selling 54p worth of this wine to your beloved customer at £8.50-ish.

Then do the calculation for a house wine costing you this time not £3 but £4:

- *Duty £1.16p*
- *VAT 60p*
- *Margin to supplier 80p*
- *Packing, freight etc. 25p*
- *Wine £1.19*
- *Total £4.00*

At 65 per cent you will charge £11.50 – not excessive these days – but the customer will be getting a wine at least twice as expensive in the making, and likely to be twice as fruity, delicious, whatever.

More creatively yet, BC can have this second, twice-as-good wine at £9.50, making you the same cash margin as not-so-good-wine-number-one, giving the customer a more pleasant experience in your hostelry.

Sample time

So, get samples – if you are able – from a variety of merchants; don't get flimflammed by discounts – look at net prices. Find six reds and six whites at your target price: if, like some publicans, you are a denizen of the cash and carry, grab a couple of bottles from them too at the same price.

Taste the wines in company – invite favoured or interested customers (who will be enormously flattered). Get someone to mask the bottles and taste them blind without fear or favour. (A good giggle is to invite a supplier to the blind tasting – will they recognise and shower praise over their wines or someone else's?) Your panel may not think of themselves as connoisseurs but they will probably come up with choices good for your punters.

If you don't want to go through this palaver and you entrust your house wine choices to a merchant, make sure that you trust both the company and their representatives further than you can throw them.

■ How creative is my 'wine by the glass' policy?

Not everyone will buy a bottle, but wine drinkers may well want more of a selection by the glass than just the house wine. Wastage of course is a worry but a vacuum stopper for the bottle is cheap, easy to use and will keep all but the frailest wines in good condition for some days.

Time is now ripe to ditch the 125ml glass. The beauty of 175ml and the cavernous 250ml glass are well known to those enjoying 40 per cent and 100 per cent uplifted profitability respectively.

DINING ROOM, APELLES CLUB

Diner: "Thomson, do the members ask for this wine?"
Head Waiter (Sotto voce): "Not twice Sir!"

■ How well are my staff trained up?

Everyone, this author included, finds it difficult to sell wine they've never tasted. If your staff have tried and hopefully enjoyed a particular wine, and have a little knowledge about it, they will enjoy selling it and seeing customers sharing the experience. Ask your supplier to come in and host a staff tasting – any good supplier will try to help and while they will not shower you with endless samples it is in their interests to support you.

The enlightened supplier may be happy to give generic wine training to your staff, which rewards them and makes them better at creating good sales. If your wine merchant produces wine lists for you, as many will, they should be able to produce a simple behind-the-bar cribsheet giving basic information on each wine for your staff to refer to.

■ Are my descriptions working hard enough for me?

The vigour and enthusiasm of the descriptions you use on lists and displays will send signals to customers about the care you take to give them access to good wines.

Press quotes too are a great aid to sales; if your list or blackboard contains a juicy Jilly Goolden quote, people tend to believe their comments rather more than those of a biased wine merchant. Also, if you are serving food, good matches with wine are a potent sales too.

Example:
Moldovan Viognier 1993 £14.95
Light and crisp with a fruity palate – medium dry.
Moldovan Viognier 1993 £14.95
By the Glass £3.50(125ml) – £3.95 (175ml) – £5.25 (250ml)

Fabulously delicate number from the cellars of Vlad Potemkin; acacia and honeysuckle on the nose followed by a dry yet honeyed body with notes of quince and violet, '. . . a minor miracle from Moldova, grab a bottle if you can!' (John Writer, Slurp Magazine); a must with our fricassée of chargrilled beetroot with banana coulis.

You see what I mean? But be sure to get it right for the culture of your establishment and for your customers. A colleague years back was so bored of writing descriptions for a particular and rather everyday wine that in artistic despair he wrote 'evokes sensations of running, naked, through verdant woods' – which might not be everyone's cup of tea.

■ How attractively do I display my wines, if at all?

When All Bar One decided its design concept, one of its great successes was to make wine visible behind the bars, attractively binned and faced, with simple but effective blackboards displaying pricing information and short descriptions. You may have a cellar full of great wine but your range will sell quicker and better if it's visible – and clearly priced – behind or around the bar.

■ Should I be prepared to list wines that are retailed to the public elsewhere?

Traditional thinking says no – out of fear that clients will work out the margins made by the proprietor. But people who are drinking decent wine aren't stupid. They know that when they buy a bottle of wine in a restaurant or bar they are likely to be paying three times what it cost and they know this applies whether or not the wine is available to the public.

Therefore the question in people's minds might be whether they'd prefer to pay this mark-up on a wine that is a) good enough to get onto shelves and b) has been publicly tasted and rated by wine journos, or one that is hidden away from such scrutiny in the depth of a merchant's cellar.

By corollary if you use a creative pricing policy on wines known to your customers (see above) they will work out that you are making less margin and in itself this could give you a distinct advantage over competitors who aren't.

Understand that when retailers retail a wine they are usually making around 30 per cent or 30p in the pound (before discounts). If they try to make much more margin the wine becomes uncommercial. The wholesaler selling unretailed wine has freedom to concoct a list price which doesn't need to be commercial but will give them the ability to discount heavily. I know of a major wholesaler whose list prices show in excess of 40 per cent or 40p in the pound.

- **Is my wine merchant bursting with creative ideas to enhance my business and are they bringing me new and interesting wines, taking an interest in my business and my customers? Are they suggesting promotions or incentive programmes?**

If the answer to these questions is 'no' it could be a subtle signal that they are not the right merchant for you. If they can't be bothered to do these things then find someone who is – perhaps a smaller, local merchant with good knowledge of your area and customer base. You may end up paying a few shillings more but the benefits of improved service will be well worth it.

Best buys

If you have addressed these questions above you are well on your way to uprating your sales and profitability. Hot areas at the moment are:

- Chile – great value, high standards and really interesting wines;
- Argentina – crunchy reds, again great value;
- France, particularly the Languedoc – some exciting wines at inexpensive prices;
- Italy – at the mid range, wines made with passion, fiercely individual and the perfect antidote to homogeneity.

Best binned

Areas to be wary of: if you insist on own-label wines (ie with your establishment's name or logo branded on the label) you are likely to have to accept compromises in the quality of the wine in the bottle, because often it is not possible to provide the best wines on this service – you may be making one step forward for your profile and two steps back on customer satisfaction.

Also beware of freebies (fridges, bunting, ice buckets, soft loans etc). They sound great but carry a cost to the merchant giving them out. If your wine merchant is giving away these goodies they are loading the costs somewhere else, and that can only be in the price of the wine.

Brands

There are also worries over branding. Australia, well on its way to becoming a dominant force in world winemaking, produces certain brands of wine which are now hugely successful in global sales. The same is true of other brands from the USA and France. When big business owns brands, the wineries behind them have to produce billions of gallons of wine to cope with the magnitude of sales and inevitably compromises need to be made.

While brands give consistency and comfort to the timid, and often big-buck support below the line, they have none of the excitement of what many think of as 'real' wines, that is, individual wine made by identifiable people, from identifiable vineyards, with passion and belief, opinion and character, with variation in style sometimes from one vintage to the next.

And if your wine merchant doesn't share the passion and excitement – there are plenty of others out there who do. Good health!

13

Lager and Beer

Danny Blyth

With the increasing importance of catering to the average pub's turnover it would be easy to neglect the possibility of making more from bulk drinking as represented by lagers and beer.

This is particularly the case when we consider how turnover and profit contribution from soft drinks, wines and coffee have been transformed from almost nothing in the last generation to become absolutely pivotal today.

A new entrant (a former restaurateur) to the trade told me recently why he has taken a local rural pub and turned it into a food house that is also looking to do much business from quality wines, waters and coffee. 'I'm looking to run dinners for business parties in my meetings room, now a private dining room, and although I could fit up to 70 in there I'll take no more than parties of 30, all looking for the complete experience,' he pledged. 'The profit from them will be super. In the old days I'd have to have 70 blokes in the bar, each having eight to 10 pints, to make the same money – and I know which group I'd rather serve and so too do my staff.'

In many ways, beer drinking is going out of fashion, let's face it. And although lager and beer are still swallowed in great quantities by a huge number of consumers, there are only a few breweries (like Fuller's, Batemans and Hop Back) bucking trends and brewing more every year.

With this in mind, and confident in the knowledge that readers have had sterling advice on matters like PPL merchandising techniques and cask beer cellarmanship and dispense tips 'up to the eyeballs', I now proffer an alternative strategy on beer, concentrating on that much ignored sector – standard strength.

MESSER

First though, confession time. After 27 years of dedicated support to pubs through the regular consumption of ales and lager, a period working on *What's Brewing*? and even being a founder member of the British Guild of Beer Writers, I have virtually given up on the grain in favour of wine and Tanqueray, when I can find it. Make of that what you will but if a diehard like me can be put off the beer genre. . .

'Ordinary' bitter

The 'stock' pump in every pub (or what most people have more often) is invariably the biggest seller. Go into deepest Wadworth Country and you'll still see most locals opting for IPA over the much bigger brand, 6X.

While the average ABV of a British ale stands at about 4.2 per cent, most people – and not just dieters or drivers having just the one – opt for the 'house' brand at about 3.7 per cent. Despite this fact, this important player rarely gets the star treatment it deserves.

Nomenclature needs attention. I feel the entire trade, from licensee and staff right back up the system through wholesaler, brewer and admen, has to drop this term 'ordinary'. This is a people issue as the term no longer appears in branding. We are collectively guilty of under-selling a top seller. Only in Britain, might the biggest seller on the menu be described as 'ordinary'. 'House bitter' won't do either. 'House' is a term for wine or aperitifs. 'Best seller' would be more accurate and relevant.

And given our liking for average strength brews it is a mistake that so few are stocked as 'guest beers'. Rare indeed is the house with even just two standard strength ales – and this also applies to 'exhibition pubs' with a dozen or more handpulls. Of course, nobody wants to be holding on to stocks of lower alcohol beers that might not remain in condition long enough to sell completely, but this problem can always be eased by cutting down on the total range, and/or using smaller cask sizes.

The real 'villain' of course is accepted practice regarding pricing and margins and this, as the entire trade knows, accounts for most guest beers coming in at about 4.2 per cent ABV. Part of this is advice from all sides in the marketing and promotional ranks to concentrate efforts on premium brands. My radical proposal is to up the price on standard strength, while stocking fewer premium and high strength brands. I have seen this employed rarely but effectively. The more people are getting what they want most and have the reasons explained as to why this is the case, the more likely they'll understand. Standard is the most popular beer – but is the demand for beer so price elastic? I doubt it.

I suspect many devotees of guest beers would love it and after all these are the customers who often consume most both in volume and in number of brands. Look at how they get just as excited about a rare 3.1 per cent mild as they do with a new 5.7 per cent strong ale. Of course, devotees like CAMRA members also make the most noise over prices (despite the high incidence of well-earning, single

Budweiser
KING OF BEERS
CRISP
CLEAN
FRESH
TRUE.
Budweiser

men in the ranks) but they are just 60,000 in number. The millions of pints of standard ale drunk every day are downed by hundreds of thousands more, people with vastly different priorities.

Standard lager

This category has been much-bashed over the years. We're familiar with the refrain: 'weak and wishy washy', 'not really American, it's brewed in Yorkshire', 'PPLs will be the death of it'. At least it's never called 'ordinary'. And still customers down it in impressive volumes.

It would be daft to argue for any price repositioning against premium lagers (as above with ale). The cash margins attainable between the two are much wider. However, there are a number of ways to use standard strength lagers as part of a strategy to improve overall customer satisfaction and this needn't mean lowering overall profits.

First there are early evening promotions. Many pubs offer price and volume deals for the early evening and after work crowds, but following the received wisdom of promoting only that which is most profitable, prefer to restrict these to premium strength brands. I'd urge a rethink. In times when there is increasing pressure for publicans to be 'socially aware', it makes little sense to get people started on 5.2 per cent lager knocked out at £1 a bottle until 7 pm. Drivers having just the one and those wanting to have a few but also to arrive home sober enough to appreciate dinner would like to take advantage of the odd promotion too. This idea seems to have taken root at lunchtimes with the likes of meal deals on a pint of Fosters and a plate of food for a certain price. Early evening might just be worth a try too.

A second idea is cultural. And it involves promoting standard lager less. I'm continually amazed at how many customers who simply ask for a pint of lager are automatically given the standard beer without further question. Smarter staff will always offer a choice, and a choice between standard and premium has the potential to make for nicely improved profits.

Today's trade is fast moving, with the rate of change increasing all the time. There is much happening in the way of soft drinks, coffee, PPSs and the like to excite the imagination. But an occasional re-appraisal of the 'old standby' lines that remain a mainstay of the business is always worthwhile.

14

Marketing Modern Day Drinks

Jonathan Dennys

My key message is: 'Increase your profits by understanding your consumers.' In an increasingly competitive market, it is more important today to focus on what will deliver sustainable profits – and how this is achieved.

At Bacardi-Martini we offer the following uncomplicated, straightforward advice on category management for all outlets, whether large or small, that management and bar staff can put into practice themselves and achieve the greatest profits.

What is category management?

'CatMan' is a simple to execute, extremely effective way of maximising sales and profitability through understanding what customers really want. The key is to translate this into providing exactly the right range of products, displayed in a way that makes it easy for them to 'shop' in the bar. This generates invaluable customer loyalty, keeping customers longer in the outlet, increasing the amount spent and therefore cash margin. The improved display encourages trial and thus increases sales of higher margin products.

'CatMan' principles also help to create and maintain higher standards of service, due to having the correct range to meet the needs of the customers. It is not, as many believe, about promoting specific products but takes a holistic

Jargon Busting

FABs – Flavoured alcoholic beverages
PPLs – Premium packaged lagers
PPSs – Premium packaged spirits
FPPS – Flavoured premium packaged spirits (overtly fruit flavoured such as Bacardi Breezer)
PPCs – Premium packaged ciders
Energy – Products such as Red Square

approach to bar profitability, optimising sales of drinks throughout the bar, meaning everyone benefits.

Why stock FABs? Pure profit in a bottle

Nowadays, every serious licensed trade outlet has a fridge behind the bar stocked with high visibility products, including flavoured alcoholic beverages (FABs). A vital element of the 'fridge' category, the FABs market is the fastest-growing alcoholic drinks sector – and certainly one of the most profitable.

What are FABs?

The market initially began in 1995 with alcocarbonates such as Hooper's Hooch, Australia's notorious Two Dogs – and a plethora of gimmicky brands. But, following public outcry, sales declined. These products began to be overtaken by the more adult and responsible premium packaged spirits (PPSs) containing a true spirit ingredient such as Bacardi Breezer or Smirnoff Ice.

The FABs market has since proven to be a dynamic and runaway success and now accounts for 35 per cent of volume of the on-trade fridge category (source: AC Nielsen, MAT Dec / Jan 2002).

The FABs category now exceeds 12.9 million cases annually and grew by over 32 per cent (volume) in the last year (source: AC Nielsen, February 2002), taking most of this share from the premium packaged lager market. With their higher average retail prices however, FABs generally offer greater returns.

Review your range

Periodic range reviews are vital to ensure you are offering the right sort of drink in the right sort of place, meaning happy customers – and bulging tills. Some products and brands sell considerably more in the summer months than the winter months and vice versa; the range should reflect this change in purchase behaviour.

Range reviews are an essential part of effective category management; a simple and effective way of maximising sales and profitability through understanding consumer needs and providing the best products in the most appealing way.

By examining your range, you can ensure products are working for your outlet, offering extra profit – and optimising valuable bar space with little or no additional outlay.

What customers want

Customers expect you to stock all the main drinks categories – and the leading names within each of these. This applies particularly to high-volume brands, such as Bacardi Carta Blanca or Smirnoff vodka.

However, while it is essential to offer the most popular brands, providing too wide a choice actually becomes confusing and counter-productive. By reducing range and clarifying the fridge, the perception is that the range has increased due to the clear product grouping.

Always ensure you're stocking the right drinks for your venue. For instance, if your bar is geared towards 'big nights out' for style-conscious 18-25 year olds, then products with 'badge values', such as Bacardi Breezer or Smirnoff Ice are essential: cheap, unknown brands will reflect badly on your outlet's image.

In the quieter, more relaxed atmosphere of a community pub, however, you should look to offer a broader range of quality ales and wines.

Profitability

The golden rule is always to look at a product's cash margin: the bigger the better! Also consider a product's gross profit per cent (GP). Work out comparative GP% on products with the following simple equation:

GP% = cash margin divided by recommended selling price (ex VAT) x 100

Remember: some products may have a lower GP%, but their cash margin (actual money in the till) could be greater due to higher rate of sale derived from their popularity.

Considerations for range reviews

Basic 'CatMan' rules

- Stock 'category signifiers' eg Smirnoff for vodka, Breezer for flavoured premium packaged spirits, Budweiser for premium packaged lagers.
- Categorise fridges and optics for a clear display.
- Use double optics where possible: additional facings attract additional sales – highlight serving suggestions such as Bacardi with Coke.
- Don't clutter the back bar area with glasses, charity boxes etc. Concentrate on displaying only what can be sold.
- Use top shelves of fridges for high margin products such as flavoured alcoholic beverages.
- Keep promotional messages clear and simple: avoid talking about price.
- Stock a range that balances profit with consumer needs.
- Maximise 'drive' products – these are 'must stock' drinks: high retail selling price / high profit margin products eg FABs, PPLs and premium draught lagers.
- Minimise 'mainstay' products – these are much lower profit margin drinks (eg draught beers and ciders).

Drink dynamics

'Demand' or 'default' products

These are drinks your customer will order, even though they can't see them, eg Budweiser. A customer will default to these when they can't see the product they really want.

'Impulse' products

These are ordered by customers who haven't decided what they want to drink; their choice can be influenced by the appeal of your range and display. Typical impulse brands would include Metz or WKD. Maximise hot spots on the back bar eg next to the tills, by building impactful display for promotional products or profitable categories.

Meeting consumer needs

As fashion and image increasingly pervade every area of life, drinks are subject to the same brand and 'badge values' as clothes and cars, particularly for younger consumers.

Premium packaged spirits are portable advertisements for their own personal image and communicate a regard for style and premium values. However, they also satisfy consumers in other ways, offering convenience, great taste and refreshment. And while other premium packaged drinks (including lager and cider) can offer these benefits too, it is only PPSs that offer the wide range of flavours and styles consumers now demand.

Driving profit

The fridge category, and flavoured alcoholic beverages (FABs) in particular, is the fastest growing area in the on-trade, and with so many new products being launched, it is vital to ensure that limited fridge space is used to its maximum potential. Thought should be given to product placement, presence and repetition of flavours.

Categories

To make 'shopping' easier for consumers (after all, your bar is your shop window), it's good practice to categorise your fridges. For example, display all your PPLs and PPCs in one fridge, all your PPSs in another, flavoured PPSs in another and so on. Brands should always be merchandised together within their category, eg all Bacardi Breezer flavours side by side in the PPS fridge.

If space limits you from individually categorised fridges, ensure shelves within a fridge are clearly categorised instead.

Baby mixers need not take up valuable fridge space – they are served with ice so do not need to be chilled.

Display

The top shelf of an under-counter fridge is the first consumers look at and should be used to display high impulse purchase products, such as new releases or flavour ranges within a single brand. Apply the same techniques to tower fridges: remember 'eye level is buy level'.

Products such as Budweiser or Smirnoff Ice have 'demand' status: consumers expect them to be available without having to see them, so they can sit on the bottom shelf.

If you have a number of fridges, ensure categories are repeated every 4–5 doors – consumers have a limited view of a busy bar so repeating them will help. It is easier for bar staff too since all categories are within easy reach.

Golden rules for the fridge:

- It's your shop window: good, impactful display is everything.
- Keep it clutter-free.
- Stock proven brand names to meet consumer demand.
- Remember: FABs are often impulse purchases, so well-stocked fridges encourage sales.
- Serve products quickly and cold to keep consumers satisfied.

Facings

Each product should have a minimum of two facings across the shelf for brand presence and more shelf space should be given to high-selling products.

Trials have shown well merchandised fridges can and will increase rate of sale by up to 30 per cent, which in turn increases profit – and it will only cost you a bit of time to get your fridges working for you!

Part 4

Selling Within Your Business

15

Importance of Marketing

Danny Blyth

Today's successful independent licensee is no stranger to marketing skills. Marketing was once something of a term of abuse in the trade but is now being deployed to great effect throughout the country, as a growing number of publicans are enacting a combined strategy of publicity, promotion and advertising on a wider stage to complement what's going on inside the business.

It is no longer exceptional to hear about a licensee coming up with a novel and quirky business idea and receiving coverage of it in the national media, print and broadcast.

Targeting

Success comes firstly through appreciation of what a combination of PR and promotion can do for trade, particularly if the initiative is finely targeted to reach the eyes and ears of a well-defined target customer.

Second comes targeting the business itself, looking at both what areas are in need of a boost and also what features may be newsworthy. Those with a clear idea about where the business is headed, such as to become more of a specialist food operation for families, tend to do best. The marketing effort is channelled efficiently with nothing else getting in the way.

The broader base local, meanwhile, needn't lose out. It too can have an underperforming part of the business boosted by publicity and promotion to a wider audience. Or it may wish to firm up its relations with the immediate community. It could also be in need of increased footfall at certain times of the trading day, or be seeking to segment itself by dedicating various rooms to facilities to appeal to a specific type of target customer.

The key message is that the marketing effort must be specialised, not the house.

Market knowledge

There's no substitute for local knowledge and the independent licensee will have a better idea than most about what makes the area tick. This is crucial in the publicity world.

First, and as an independent, you will be largely free to talk to the local media and develop your own special relationship. Big retail chains have their arms tied and mouths gagged most of the time. You must make this advantage pay off.

Second, while the big boys can call upon demographic socio-economic research statistics, the independent licensee will know the trading area intimately and probably for a long while. He will also know what sort of initiatives have both worked and failed in the past. This is another advantage to exploit.

If, however, you need some more detailed research in relation to development at the pub that entails a big investment, then your local authority should be able to furnish you with some socio-economic background, most probably through the department responsible for economic development or attracting business into the area. Other data can be sourced from the Small Business Unit of the Department of Trade and Industry (tel 020 7215 5000). Should your business involve tourism then the British Tourist Authority (tel 020 8846 9000) can assist. Help and advice is available on publicity and sometimes funding too.

Finally there's the tried and tested means of visiting the competition; not just rival pubs but other businesses competing with you for the local leisure pound – everything from cinemas through to restaurants. Gaps in the market can be identified, ideas taken and adapted for your own use.

Publicise

Making ready

Just by taking marketing seriously you are on the way. Relying on word of mouth might involve less time, budget and energy but it can be a long haul. Effective promotion can show a return much more quickly. In a short space of time, existing customers could be spending more and potential customers will be lured in for the first time.

Winning combinations

A pub with successful marketing relies on a combination of resources being employed both internally and externally. Good internal marketing is the essential starting point, in everything from eye-catching menus and tempting dish or wine descriptions. Regular promotions also play a crucial role, and external marketing must follow.

Free PR through the local newspaper cannot work alone. Advertising, which again can prove extremely effective, also needs something else. And that something else is the sum of the combined effort: promotion, PR, marketing and publicity. A new development which affects all of these is the use of information technology in making the business run better. The remainder of this section now looks at each of these issues.

16

Winning Promotions

Elton B. Mouna

Resist temptation. This should be the first rule in promotions. By temptation I mean the urge to transfer that belief of yours, that your pub is a business, and so promotions should always be hard-headed affairs solely focused on the biggest of brands with the bottom line the lone measure of success.

Customer focus

To your customer the pub isn't so much a business, rather a place to meet friends and enjoy themselves. They don't want to feel part of a business or promotions plan while there. Everything I do on the promotions front here at Fullers has this customer priority to the fore. And it's working to good effect. It is an old saying but a saying nonetheless that I remind myself of daily: 'The customer is King.' The customer truly is King.

Customer expectation

Not all promotions have to be 'all singing all dancing' affairs. I believe many small types of activity, something always happening, add up to one great pub. Customers should leave your pub thinking, 'I love that pub, I don't know why, but I do.' In reality they love it because there are always lots of little things happening.

You will want, and will need, to run bigger events. Again remember customer expectation. Never over-promise. Never over-promote. In some instances it might even help to underplay things. If people arrive expecting a grand show and all they find is a good, but not great night, 20p off drinks and the odd person winning a pen or T-shirt, they'll feel let down. If they arrive not having been led to expect too much – and then do enjoy themselves – they will depart much happier.

You can then start to evolve. A successful pub has got to evolve. And this is best done through a gradual succession of events. Learn what your customer wants and learn through trial and error how to deliver it.

Working with suppliers

Suppliers can be of great help with promotions through provision of product and other support. What you must do here is ensure that your event does actually result in sales of their product. You shouldn't take without giving.

Establish a track record of shifting their product and you can then ask – and receive – more in the future. By the same token impress on suppliers that both the pub and the customer has to see something from a promotion.

You can also work with suppliers to develop targeted promotions that help set you off against the competition, which too often are locked into old style BOGOF ('Buy One Get Free') type offers.

Applying a modern twist to an old promotion can add flair. Working with suppliers to create tailor-made promotions can be hard work but it can be rewarding. For instance you could try 'Buy None Get One Free.' I did this among our local public services like hospital, fire and ambulance, writing to each in the post-Christmas period thanking them for their work over the festive season. While the nation ate turkey and relaxed, the services worked hard. I supplied each of them with 'Buy None Get One Free' vouchers. Each voucher entitled then to a complimentary drink of their choice supplied by our suppliers. This was a nice thing to do, improving the pub and Fuller's image. It also brought new customers into the pubs – employed, responsible people who left the pub feeling good about it, the brand and the company too. Chances of repeat purchase, increased brand loyalty and repeat custom improved too. Again, customer, brand (supplier) and pub all have to benefit.

There's a number of other twists to old themes that might just work for you – what about a grumpy hour instead of a happy hour? It could feature a picture of you, a dejected looking landlord, with the strapline: 'It might make you happy but boy it makes him grumpy' followed by the list of price reductions. This is a great example of that little something different that makes your customers think, 'I love that pub, I don't know why, I just love it!' A happy hour is not a talking point. A grumpy hour is.

Brands: big and small

On the theme of lots of different things happening and my one crusade to re-invent that awful phrase 'Buy One Get One Free', I recently ran a promotion called 'Buy

GRUMPY HOUR
IT MIGHT MAKE YOU HAPPY BUT IT SURE MAKES HIM GRUMPY!
THE MANAGER
PINT OF LONDON PRIDE, STELLA, CARLING OR GUINNESS
BOTTLE OF SMIRNOFF ICE - GLASS OF HOUSE WINE
all £2
MONDAY & TUESDAY
4PM UNTIL CLOSING

Rum Get Rum Free'. A simple twist on a double Bacardi for the price of a single. Simple stuff but it got people talking and it sold the rum.

How about a promotion that simply gives the customers a little more for their money? I ran an exceptionally successful promotion in conjunction with our suppliers called 'Quantity Surveyors'. Here customers were offered the large version of a drink, from a full range, for the price of a small serving. For example a large Pepsi for the price of a smaller serving, a 250ml glass of wine for the price of 175 ml glass.

However, you needn't restrict promotions to the big brands alone. By using some of the smaller brands across the range of drinks, from beers and lagers through soft drinks and on to spirits and mixed drinks you are establishing a varied and interesting promotions programme. And you are keeping your back bar area lively and attractive, always with something new to grab customers' attention.

Mixing it

Looking to the future I can see a bright future for mixed drinks. Why look for the elusive next bottled alcopop or premium package spirit when you can mix your own premium spirits with premium mixers, something like Bombay Sapphire with cranberry juice topped up with lemonade. Very simple but very good. It can be served quickly, by anyone behind the bar, yet it can be served with flair. Presented well it can give the customer exactly what is required and priced correctly it can give you an excellent margin. It also gives you a point of difference.

High standards

No matter what your idea for promotions, however, never lose sight of the fact that what is most guaranteed to get customers coming back is having high standards in all areas of your operations. Don't start promoting your pub until you are happy with your standards. Promoting your pub whilst operating with, shall I say, mixed standards, will only highlight your faults. Set standards high and maintain them and then promote your pub. Not the other way round.

High standards also apply to the quality of welcome too. It really is the sum of lots of smaller things that go together to make for customers having an enjoyable time. It is therefore best to avoid some of the mandatory 'upselling' promotional techniques used by some of the larger pub companies like asking the customer if he'd like any nuts or crisps with his drink. Once you've been asked – and refused – more than once you become fed up. It's better to concentrate more on promoting snack sales through measures like sampling or else 'hot spotting' on the back bar display.

On a similar vein, while out enjoying a meal many customers find their enjoyment impaired by being subject to a barrage of promotional offers while they are out to unwind.

THE QUEEN'S GOLDEN JUBILEE 2002
BUY A MEAL
GIVE A CROWN
FOR EVERY PURCHASE OF
SAUSAGES & MASH, FISH & CHIPS
OR STEAK & ALE PIE
FULLER'S WILL DONATE 25P TO BARNARDOS
(THAT'S A CROWN IN OLD MONEY!)
BARNARDOS IS ONE OF THE QUEEN'S CHOSEN
GOLDEN JUBILEE CHARITIES
FULLERS
OFFER VALID FROM
SATURDAY 1ST JUNE - SUNDAY 9TH JUNE INCLUSIVE
Barnardos

Food promotion

Look for alternative promotions such as simply letting people know about your food offer. Do something like photograph what you have to sell and reproduce this on a leaflet to be posted through letter boxes saying to people, 'We're proud of what we have to offer – why not come and try it for yourself.' Consider building in an incentive as part of this package. Or you could focus promotion on filling the dining area more during its quieter times by targeting customer groups like the elderly. Try theme nights like Indian Curry Nights or Italian Nights if these suit your style of catering operation. Remember this. Some pubs serve all their food with chips; serve all your food with flair.

Promote food in an on-going way by simple things like providing a free cake for a customer on his birthday – or keeping a 'birthday database' and sending out a card in advance of the day so that they are encouraged to come to your pub for their celebration. Promotion needn't be large scale, nor need it involve high spend. This is especially true with the smaller, personal touches which create a lot of goodwill. And all my customers wear metaphorical crowns.

Providing there is a good customer focus, promotions should never go far wrong. And if you are to be a tad more ambitious ensure you don't lose sight of the value of the customer in whatever you do. The real trick is to retain this 'house standard' while also getting something out of it for the pub itself and any brand that may be on board.

Look after the customer and the pub looks after itself.

Part 5

Selling Your Business Outside

17

Publicity and Self-promotion

Danny Blyth

Though we're all quite fed up with spin doctors – you shouldn't let that sour you. Learning some more about the art of publicising your pub is a cost-effective means of marketing that can reap some big rewards.

Although the old maxim of all publicity being good publicity doesn't entirely apply to the pub situation (few would welcome a drugs bust or shooting on the premises), well managed publicity can build trade on any number of fronts. At its base level it spreads the message about what your business has to offer, what makes it distinct and what makes it good, and it takes this message to a wider audience of potential customers.

Media know-how

First, acquaint yourself with the media that are read, listened to and watched by your target customer. See what sort of stories and features they cover, think opportunities all the time.

Try to develop some sort of relationship with journalists in that media. Target individual journalists. Try asking them down to your pub for a drink. Discuss the sort of stories they cover and how it's best to get information to them and in what form. This will be easy with the local paper but very difficult with specialist national distribution magazines and the like. But through starting simply you'll begin to master techniques you can apply elsewhere.

Once you do have a story to tell, call up either your known contact or the news desk. Prepare a concise outline of what you have to say and be prepared to note requests for further information. Get back quickly with the details asked for.

You might also find it useful to have prepared a news release, which is a brief report of a story, detailing either what's going to happen or what has taken place. Keep it short, keep to the point, ensuring your story tells the news editor 'who, where, what, why and when'. Most releases ramble or else fail to excite and that's why most end up in the bin. However, those received in good time and telling a good story clearly and without exaggerated glitz, are favourites to make it into print. And always follow the established rules:

- Use plain white paper, headed in capitals 'News Release'.
- Get your story printed on a PC printer, using double spacing.
- Keep to a single sheet of paper.
- Be accurate with details like times, dates and names.
- End with a 'contact for further information' and telephone number.
- Send in good time to meet the deadline.

In the meantime there are several opportunities for free publicity there for the taking. See first the listings or 'What's On' sections of papers and magazines, student publications or those of special interest groups you'd like to attract to the pub. Ensure you first talk to the person responsible for putting that section together and determine how they like to receive details and when. Other free opportunities for coverage come through offering your services for guest articles and through letters columns. Be sparing with this though – people loathe those they view as pushy.

Also consider reviews of pubs and eating places that appear. Find out who puts them together and how you could feature.

Human interest stories are regular winners, so if you've done something good for the local community or particularly unfortunate individuals, or if your staff have achieved something special, seek to use the story for positive press coverage.

Making news

You can devise your own news. Work on an idea that is based around a good story and suits a good photograph. Ensure the story allows you to publicise a part of your business and fits in with the style of your operation. You could mark historical connections with the pub, or think up a new annual competition or community event.

Latch on to what is already in the news: elections, royal weddings, Wimbledon etc. Put a local twist on things – that's what the local newspaper editor is looking for most with breaking news.

You could try getting listed in any of the multitude of guide books that are published covering pubs, beer, food, family welcome, accommodation etc. Again, target a publication, first finding out whether entry is paid for or through nomination (always the better option). You can often nominate yourself. Free entry, independent guide books can often bring in valuable extra business and they remain on the shelves doing that job for a year. Gaining an entry for the first time in a particularly prestigious publication is always good cause for announcing the news in the local media.

Winning awards

Winning an award should always make for good business-building fodder. It's a good local news story and one that associates your pub with excellence.

Society today is fast becoming 'awards mad' and this includes pubs. There are awards for pub food, family friendliness and many other features of the business. Look out for opportunities in the trade press, local, regional and national media. You'll be spoilt for choice.

And there are other benefits to winning apart from the glory of it all and the trade building effect. Winning improves team spirit among staff, improves relations with suppliers and even goes down well with the bank manager. Professionally it's a sign that you're on the right lines.

Making your case

Making a good case is vital. This starts with choosing the right awards for your business – one where you stand a chance and where winning should help you meet a business goal. Then choose the right category, the one where you are strongest. Remember you can usually enter more than one category, but be sparing in this as each makes quite some demands on your time.

Don't be discouraged if you lose out. Try and try again, making an improved case each time.

Don't rush to fill in the entry form. Photocopy it several times and work on a few drafts, taking your time to consider a good, succinct case majoring on all those points the entry materials say judges are looking for. Use the option to add further information if necessary but always keep things short and to the point. Complete the original entry form in clear handwriting, free of spelling errors.

Attach fresh copies of supporting printed matter, like menus, pub brochure, promotional flyers. If supplying photographs get a set of quality shots taken by a professional – it may be expensive but your case will be so much stronger and you can always use copies for future promotional purposes. Finally, post it in good time before the deadline after making a copy for future reference.

Shortlisting

Pubs shortlisted for awards are usually visited by a journalist who will write a profile of you and your business for publication, plus make notes for use by the judging panel. Improve your chances by:

- re-familiarising yourself with your entry form;
- preparing for expected questions in relation to your entry criteria;
- restricting your answers to points in support of your entry;
- planning a complete 'tour' of your business ahead of the visit – where to go, what to show, what people to meet;
- being relaxed and welcoming and confident in your case.

Don't overdo the entertaining or the drink. But do look after the visitor, who might well turn out to become a long-term media contact. Provide good overnight accommodation and make the effort to pick somebody up from the station.

Judging panels

If shortlisted you might be asked to appear before a judging panel. Again, prepare well by bringing along your entry form and copies of material supplied. Anticipate areas of questioning. Rehearse the key points you wish to get over, keeping them to hand in note form as bullet points.

Things to avoid are being nervous (easy to say) and reading from a script (easy to reject). Consider too possible weaknesses in your case and address these in advance. And always speak clearly and maintain eye contact, being yourself as much as possible.

Winning times

Ensure as many people as possible hear about it should you win. Begin with your staff and customers and carry on with suppliers, and everyone else you deal with. Post the news on your website then get busy telling the local media, newspapers, TV and radio.

You might care to host a party to celebrate, inviting along all those people you have broken the news to and where you will unveil the trophy. Plan a variety of 'photo opportunities' for media who come along, get copies and display them at the pub afterwards. Put the news on posters facing outside, on an exterior banner or A-board. Include the news on all printed promotional matter you produce. Everybody likes a good news story.

18

Using Technology to Develop Profit

Patrick Dardis

The 'e' word seems to be on the lips of every licensee I meet these days. Nothing to do with drugs, I hasten to add, but e-commerce, or electronic commerce, to be more precise. More and more licensees are turning to information technology to help their business, whether it's for ordering goods, emailing customers or accessing trade information via the Internet.

I have been in the pub business for over 20 years and always felt that sooner or later the trade would have to grasp the nettle and embrace this technology, despite its deeply traditional ways. A colleague and I had considered setting up some sort of online system that would improve the way licensees order their goods and manage their businesses. Sadly, it didn't materialise back then, but when I received a call from Grey Archer, one of a handful of companies targeting the pub industry with its own online package, it was a challenge I couldn't resist. Now I find myself developing new ideas for a company that is at the leading edge of a revolution in the pub trade.

Grey Archer (sponsor of this chapter) was launched in September 2001 and currently has over 1000 members paying a £40 monthly subscription for which they receive a PC, colour printer, software installation, free one-to-one training and access to a range of suppliers of food, drink and ancillary products on their online ordering system. Special offers on utilities and a series of add-on discounted packages are available, as is a technical support line 16 hours a day, seven days a week.

To change the ways licensees do business is no easy task. I have seen things from both sides of the bar, as a director of national and regional pub companies and also pulling pints in a south-west London pub.

In those days, many licensees adopted the 'fag packet' system – jotting down their order requirements on the back of a cigarette packet so that when a supplier's sales call came they knew how many bags of crisps and barrels of beer they needed. Those same licensees would throw their receipts into a shoebox, ready to hand over to their accountants at end of year.

One thing that always amazed me was how licensees would often do their stock count in the middle of the night after a busy shift, deciding *then* what they needed to order in the way of drinks and dry goods.

Not all licensees work like that of course. Others check stock first thing in the morning. But in all cases, they would wait for a telesales girl to phone and take the order, at which time they might be down the cellar or, for the privileged few, on the golf course. With an online ordering exchange, things are different.

Online ordering lets licensees place orders with a wider range of suppliers and at their own convenience, not the suppliers'. They can organise their lives, choosing to place orders last thing at night, in the small hours or in the light of day, and our research shows that people do all of the above. No more waiting for telesales calls and no more traipsing to the cash and carry several times a week.

PC packages

There's more to technology, though, than simply ordering online. The PC has a variety of uses. It provides access to the Internet and email and can be used to create financial packages, databases, menus, posters and advertisements. One thing that always annoyed me in pubs was the state of their handwritten posters, dog-eared and scruffy. Certainly in recent years, licensees have woken up to the fact that a computer enables them to create and print material with a real professional look, not the 'hastily-put-together-after-a-busy-trading-session' look!

Legislation

Licensees can also access accounting software to calculate profit margins and download important legal documents, which would normally have to be sourced in written form. Dealing with legal matters is one area that I know licensees find increasingly difficult. Legislation is changing all the time, with working time directives, the minimum wage, National Insurance and a whole mass of other red tape with which to cope.

In the past, unless licensees kept abreast of developments through the trade papers or by way of their business manager, they wouldn't know what was happening. Now, they can be alerted either via email from legal service providers or through a growing number of trade-related websites.

Communication

Information is certainly one area that I can see continuing to develop as the trade gets increasingly fragmented. With pub sell-offs and ex-managed pubs going to tenancy or lease, licensees have to plough their own furrow a lot more. They don't have the sort of close relationship they used to enjoy with their brewery company.

Ease of use

This is where the PC and the Internet will play a key role in the future. Almost every home has a PC these days, but our research shows that less than 30 per cent of the country's 65,000 licensees have one, and even fewer in the independent sector. For some, the cost of hardware is a factor and many are reluctant to invest in equipment with which they are not familiar and don't believe they will ever master. But those who don't join the computer revolution will certainly lag behind in the future.

One of the main comments I hear from licensees logging on for the first time is that they wish they'd done so years ago. Many licensees had mistakenly thought they had to be some sort of computer whiz-kid, but in reality found that a computer required no high-tech skills and got to grips with the system in a very short time.

Not high-tech

No one is suggesting that the computer is the answer to all of a licensee's problems. A licensee should not expect Nirvana and those new to the system will naturally experience teething problems. But we have found that even the most die-hard licensees who are steeped in tradition and reluctant to change their ways are soon able to navigate their way round the keyboard like seasoned professionals. Often it is merely fear of the unknown that holds people back.

Marketing key

A licensee who wants to increase his business, but struggles against cut-price chains like Wetherspoon, will find the computer an increasingly useful marketing tool.

I have worked with pubs aimed at the student market, which I believe have led the way in developing PC usage as a way of attracting more customers. These licensees realised that many of their customers and potential customers had access to computers at their colleges or universities and that their target market was out there to be reached.

They quickly set up websites listing their pub's facilities, stories of fame or historical interest, special events and promotional offers. They then invited customers to enter online prize draws to win drinks, or whatever, asking them to give their email addresses for data capture purposes. The pub would soon have a database of hundreds of target customers at its disposal for the next event or new product launch or promotion.

Websites

Developing a pub website is a great way to market the business. And again, those worried that they don't have the computer know-how to set up a database or think it's going to cost a fortune to create a website are mistaken. Help is readily available via Internet providers and there's no shortage of companies willing to give advice.

Promotions

The web promotional ideas are limitless. Meal deals, drinks offers, birthday greetings, happy hours and so on. Pubs with bedrooms can link their sites to tourist boards and accommodation providers, allowing potential customers from near and far to view the facilities and even book online. Pubs with food offerings can entice ramblers to see what's on the menu for a mid-walk stop!

Many licensees are downloading quiz questions from the Internet and viewing new pub properties to buy online. There's one licensee I know who runs a type of matchmaking service by putting pictures of female customers on the site and getting the boys to vote for their 'girl of the month'.

I know of many pubs whose businesses have substantially increased through their own email databases and websites, and can't believe that 70 per cent of licensees still have no email address and very few pubs have websites.

Training

If it saves time and money, then it's got to be good. But there's no substitute for one-to-one training for new members of staff, right? Not quite. The PC can help in the area of staff training – but without actually replacing that essential personal contact. Specialised interactive CD-ROMs enable staff to undergo their basic training on the computer, which can be done during quiet times in the pub. This, of course, is coupled with hands-on training behind the bar or in the kitchen, but it frees up valuable hours for the licensee who would otherwise have to sit down with the staff member and laboriously plough through workbooks.

Loyalty

Technology lets pubs get closer to their customers. From big operators like Scottish & Newcastle to smaller independents, pubs can run loyalty schemes that capture customer data via swipe cards. Card-reading terminals are linked to a pub's EPOS

(Electronic Point of Sale), allowing licensees to give discounts and offers when they swipe customers' loyalty cards.

As well as being a very efficient till system, EPOS allows licensees to monitor their business on an ongoing basis. At the touch of a button they can see which lines are selling, which aren't and where the business is heading. Conventional till systems do not highlight problem areas and it may be too late when an accountant runs the rule over the books. EPOS gives instant access to the figures.

Any licensees preparing to invest in either EPOS or a loyalty scheme should make sure the system they choose has the facility to take a smart card. At Grey Archer, we offer EPOS, card swipe, mobile top-up and other electronic digital systems as add-ons to our package.

Digital developments

Digital and satellite technology is set to play an ever-increasing part in a pub's entertainment package, whether it's big screen television, background music or jukebox. After all, consumers have the latest technology and top quality sound systems at home these days. They don't want to go to the pub to find music crackling out of a cassette recorder through battered old speakers or they will soon go elsewhere.

We are already seeing the introduction of Internet-based gaming machines, jukeboxes and other digital packages, making the need for a digital line even more important. Customers want to play the latest games on the latest games machines, and these are increasingly being provided digitally and via the Internet. Licensees need this kind of equipment if they are to stay ahead of the competition.

The Internet is continually getting quicker and more user-friendly. There may have been a lot of resistance to technology in the past, but those coming on board are really seeing the benefits – saving time and money and finding they can't do business without it.

Part 6

Key Customer Groups

19

The Youth Market

Dominic Roskrow

If you're thinking about making a positive move to attract the youth market, then you might want to take the advice of one leading pub company chief executive. When asked for one piece of advice he smiled and said: 'don't bother.' And if you're determined to press ahead anyway, then the next piece of advice is: 'Do so, but with extreme caution.'

Successfully ensnaring the youth market is the holy grail of the drinks trade. The under 35s tend to be young, free and often single, they tend to have a high level of disposable income, they tend to go out more and stay out longer, and they're very brand aware. More than that they're prepared to invest substantial sums of money paying top prices to make sure they're in the right environment and that they're seen with the right product.

But catching the youth market is like surfing: you have to pick your moment, ride the fashion wave for as long as you can stay on it, then get off, start again and try and pick the next roller coaster.

It's not only a difficult market to get to grips with, it's a fickle and fast-changing one, and it is ruthless and unforgiving. Get your offering wrong and you could drive any regular clientele you had away and have nothing to replace it with. And even if you get it right you will eventually have to make a stark choice between evolving your outlet to keep hold of the youth you have as they grow older, or abandoning them for the next generation of party-goers.

For the simple fact remains; one person's trendy haunt is his younger brother's idea of an old fogies' bar. The chances are you are going to struggle to be all things to everybody. But there are ways that different markets can co-exist in your pub.

In essence this means clearly segregating time within your venue and advertising the fact that you are doing so.

If you decide, for instance, that every Thursday, Friday and Saturday night will be aimed at the 18–30 year old market, you must advertise that fact well to both older customers and younger ones. You need a clear point at which the evening changes, and an hour before that time arrives the music should be taken up a notch and made more lively, and the lighting adjusted accordingly.

This will subtly encourage the day time clientele to leave the pub without being made to feel unwelcome. None of this is easy and takes a great deal of time and effort.

If you do decide to go ahead with it, anyway, then there are plenty of positive reasons why you might want to do so beyond the financial. Vibrant lively and youthful venues are fun places to be, they create a momentum of their own, and they allow the operator to be flamboyant and experimental. Hard work – but fun hard work.

Research your subject

Before you do anything, research your subject carefully. Visit bars in your area and take note of what they're stocking; compile a list of opposition outlets, and note any unusual features or points of difference they have.

Seek advice from as many different sources as you possibly can. Talk to all your drinks suppliers about popular brands and make sure you stock them. Consider commissioning a street survey and ask youngsters where they go out, and why they go there.

Stock the right brands

It's not hard to find out the brands young drinkers want most, and 80 per cent of your stock will stay fairly constant. Brands such as Stella, Kronenbourg, Beck's etc have reached icon status and are unlikely to fall by the wayside on the whim of fashion. But being prepared to stock new brands and fad brands and react quickly when the trends move on is very important.

Get the music right

Don't make the mistake of thinking you can do this for yourself. Music is probably the most important single factor when getting a young person's venue right, and the hardest to do well.

The best way of getting this right is to bring in outside help. Find who the trendiest DJs are and talk to them about hosting club nights in the pub and advising on other nights. The modern DJ will have his own following and although it will cost you to use him, you'll guarantee an audience and he'll be able to provide you with instant credibility.

You will be able to negotiate all sorts of deals. Allow him to advertise his gigs through fly posters and he'll undoubtedly repay the compliment.

Embrace technology

Without getting too insulting about it, today's youngsters have the attention span of a gnat and demand to be entertained constantly. Music isn't enough. The more television screens or video walls you have, the better. Internet and quiz machines are all but essential, and on-screen promotions will go down particularly well.

Technology is most appreciated among youngsters when it is being used for promotional purposes. Telephone texting is one of the best ways to involve customers and to drive trade.

A number of texting companies are in the market place and will be able to do everything from just informing customers of a special drinks offer to linking customers up for playing quizzes or even pub dating.

You can build a comprehensive database from the information that customers submit and can use it to send text messages offering anything from a free birthday drink to information on your next major event.

In one case a pub offered a text voucher to customers – all the recipient had to do was go to the bar at a certain time and show the text message to get a free drink. It brought in 65 extra customers on a Monday night. Drinks suppliers promoting a new product will only be too happy to help with such a promotion.

Get the food offering right

Go for simple snack style foods such as wraps, burgers, nachos and so on. And try to offer something easy but a bit different. One pub in the South-West has started offering omelettes with a variety of sweet and savoury toppings. At weekends that's all they offer – and they have seen food turnover rocket.

Have high profile promotions

Encourage tasting nights, get the drinks companies bringing in new products, and where you get the chance, make sure your pub is used for key competitions or promotions around big sporting events. If you can attract in the major drinks companies they will do much of the hard work for you by providing people to give out the drinks and the promotional material to make sure the event is a success.

Attract women

Offer bottles of wine or Bacardi Breezers at half price before a certain time, or hold a silly event aimed at women. The fact remains that even in this day and age groups of women will attract groups of men. Making your pub female-friendly is therefore essential.

Consider gimmicks

Tacky as it might be, many of them work. Fancy condom machines, a good selection of cigarettes, a bottles-only serving hatch and spirits dispensed manually are all easy and effective ways of adding a touch extra to your pub offering.

Listen to your customers

Ask your customers either directly or indirectly what they want from the pub and what they would like to see you offer. In this way they will feel that they have an ownership stake in the pub.

Remember the basics

Perhaps most importantly of all, remember what type of pub you are and don't lose sight of that. One of the advantages you have over your opposition is that you are a pub, and often many of the more traditional aspects of your establishment placed alongside new one are what makes it so attractive. Cask ale, for instance, can enjoy a healthy following among younger drinkers.

The youth market is always looking for somewhere else to go and something new to do. The skill of catering for that market is reinventing yourself so that they constantly feel there is something new about your offering.

It's a tough nut to crack, but with enough foresight, hard work and planning, the 18–35 year old market can be catered for, and the benefits are massive.

But remember – know your limits and never stop surfing.

20

Families

Dominic Roskrow

There has rarely been a better time than now for taking a bold step forward to attract the family market.

For while it might seem that the independent publican is at a massive disadvantage when trying to compete against the national chains and their multi-million pound family dining restaurants, this isn't the case at all.

In actual fact those monoliths are actually burdened by their size and inflexibility. They're predictable and unimaginative. And they're looking increasingly tired. But most important of all from a small operator's point of view, they're becoming outdated.

Indeed it would be no exaggeration to say that the United Kingdom is at a major crossroads when it comes to providing a pub environment for the whole family. The big chain establishments might eventually choose the right direction to go in, but by then a forward-thinking independent outlet could have sprinted way ahead and carved out its own unique family venue.

The simple fact is that venues with piles of chip meals and carbonated drinks, standard beer offering and average wine where the kids are thrown in to a cage full of coloured balls and climbing equipment just won't cut it any more. Millions have been pumped in to them and the independent can't compete with them – and shouldn't want to. For increasingly parents are growing bored with the idea of getting rid of the children for as long as it takes for an older kid to sit on them or push them off the rope ladder.

There is a herd mentality about such places – and parents have had enough. The crossroads we have reached stems from the growth in awareness of Europe in general, and from the prevalence of Continental cafe venues in Britain in particular.

More than this, many pubs have opened their doors to children not because they want them, but because they need them. Families make good business sense but it's not enough to tolerate the little ones – you've got to welcome them.

Look different

The future family pub might not be about cheap food at all. Have it, yes. Be imaginative and flexible, offer healthy options for children, and try and offer as much of the main menu in adult form as you can.

The key to your success in this area will be by not competing with the big chains but making it very clear from the outside of your pub that families are welcome. Garden equipment is an obvious visible way of doing this. Modern brightly-coloured climbing apparatus and a larger investment than just a couple of swings is a clear indication to a parent that they can enjoy their time in your pub garden because the children are going to be happy. Any activities that turn your garden in to a party venue will immediately appeal to families.

Seek out help if you can, too. If you know of a three or four mile walk that can start and end at your pub, then seek out local pub walks guides and get your pub included. It's amazing how popular pub walks are for families, and how many modern parents treat themselves and their offspring to a treat when they have stretched their legs!

Getting it right

There are three general rules that any potential outlet intending to market to families needs to establish right from the start:

- If the words 'little brat' come to mind when you see a three year old, you need to reassess your position.
- Don't try and compete with the national food restaurants. Treat them as inverted blueprints – guides as to not how to do things.
- Target the parents, of course, but target children more.

This last point is crucial if you are going to succeed in attracting sustainable family business. Children are astoundingly marketing- and brand-literate, and the big companies know it. Turn the television on to kids TV at 5pm and you'll see advertising aimed straight at the toddler. They know exactly what they want from three and fully understand logos at six.

Providing the ideal family venue that will work in the years ahead requires meeting the needs of both parents and their children. For while it is true that most children love ball parks up to a point, the concept of dumping your offspring somewhere so you can get on with relaxing over lunch is peculiarly British and increasingly outdated. And children eventually get fed up of the whole shebang.

The future for family dining lies in involving children in the eating out experience, in entertaining them and in making them feel special. This doesn't need to mean great expense and it doesn't mean abandoning your pub to packs of horrific dribbling toddlers. Almost the opposite, in fact.

The European factor

An increasing number of parents have seen the way children are integrated into dining occasions across Europe. And they want the same sort of thing here.

The history of this country and of the pub within it has meant that the experience of children here is very different. Our complicated laws haven't helped. But no matter what the reason, it would be unthinkable to enter a bar or restaurant in France or Italy and be presented with a list of rules governing children.

Furthermore, it is exceedingly rare to find children running around and screaming their heads off when out with their parents in Europe, and yet that's exactly what we have traditionally encouraged from them here by throwing them in to a play area.

In Europe children are welcomed in to an adult environment and expected to act in a certain way as a result.

That doesn't mean anyone should expect children to be angels. They shout a lot. They cry a lot. They spill food all over the floor. Take issue with that and you're likely to provoke one of only two reactions from the parents – embarrassment, or annoyance that you've got a problem with their darling offspring. In both cases they won't come back in the short-term, and your reputation as a family outlet will be destroyed soon afterwards.

But while tolerance in this manner is essential, insisting on respect for your outlet is important, too. No other guest should have to suffer someone else's children, no one should have to risk having their pint spilled because the bar has become a running track, and no parent should feel that they can let their children run riot when those children are being treated as grown ups.

Talking to children

The key to making your pub a haven for families spending quality time is making the children feel special. Encourage your staff to talk directly to the children, asking them what they want and offering them choices.

Simple tactics work. It's a good idea to have as wide a choice of soft drinks as possible, covering everything from cherryade to mango juice. And why not invest in some children's cups and let them choose what they drink from? It's a cheap tactic but highly effective – every child eating with you has from the outset been made to feel special and because he or she has a cup like no one else, you've made them unique.

Encourage your staff to ask the name of toys children bring in, or to enquire about presents if it's a birthday. Keep a selection of treats to give out to good children, and subtly bribe them from the outset by letting them know there will be a treat at the end of the meal. It doesn't always work because children are unpredictable, but where possible strike up a rapport with the child. If Daddy wants another drink, for instance, ask the child if he should be allowed to. All this costs nothing more than time, and it's the sort of thing that the big chains, with all their pressure and the need for quick turnover, fail miserably with.

Keeping them amused

You don't need to spend thousands on amusement, nor should you because the big chains will always be able to spend more. But neither is it enough to stick them down at a table with a handful of broken crayons and a couple of pieces of paper to scribble on.

But a little bit of creativity can work wonders, particularly if you can think of something to amuse children that is unique to your pub. Its history, geographic location and the community it's situated in are all possible subject matters. But here are a few ideas that have successfully been used by pubs in this country.

Quizzes

Design a quiz about the pub that either requires answering questions while seated or which gives scope for adults to accompany children around the pub looking for clues.

Stories

If your pub has a gruesome and exciting history, get someone from the local paper or in the community to write the stories up. If there's someone handy with computer graphics or illustrations, rope them in too. The more stories and the gorier, the better – children love to hear about ghosts, smuggling, wars, killing, highwaymen and so on. You could even sell booklets for a few pence to reward the contributors, or use the proceeds for a local charity. Alternatively, provide the books free for parents to read before meals.

Involve children

It takes little effort to provide a salad bar and to encourage children to choose their own salad accompaniments. If you're more adventurous, let children come to a pizza table and assemble their own pizzas before taking them away to cook them. Not only does it engage the children but they're more likely to eat a meal they think they've prepared. Fruit salads lend themselves to the same sort of thing.

Herb gardens

Greene King's Appletons concept came up with the idea of adding herbs to children's recipes and having a herb garden where children could smell the herbs, learn a bit about them and then taste them in their cooking. It's different, it's fun and it's educational.

Challenges

If you do have a special children's room or area, challenge children to see how high they can build a Lego stack, or something similar. If there's a historic or haunted element to the pub, encourage children to enter a weekly drawing competition – they draw the picture and leave the details, and they win £20 off the next family meal, or something similar.

Entertainers

It might be a bit tacky getting someone dressed as a bear wandering through the pub, but the odd visit from a pirate or history figure becomes an event for children and at weekends particularly it's worth the effort. Face painting is another highly popular children's activity and you should be able to come to some arrangement with somebody over it. And if you know anyone who can make balloon shapes or do a short performance to entertain children, even better.

Summer parties

Barbecues provide ideal children's food ideas, and a jazz band in the garden with a selection of a summery drinks can become a real talking point.

Toilet facilities

In this day and age fathers are as responsible for nappy duties as mothers, so try and provide an area where both parents can go to change their children. The least you should be offering is a small table with a soft mat on it, or a wall-mounted changing table. Extras such as paper towels, wipes and paper nappies (even for a small charge) will set you ahead of a great many of your competitors.

Summary

To successfully attract families can be relatively easy and cheap. You need to make an effort, accommodate families fully and not just tolerate them, set out to make them feel special and offer them something they're unlikely to get elsewhere.

Build up a database of family names, addresses and birthdays. For the price of a cheap birthday card, a stamp and a small offer – one free children's meal, for instance – you can establish yourself as a caring, family-friendly venue. And once you've done that, word of mouth will do the rest. After all, have you ever seen mums chatting as they wait for their children outside nursery, play group or school?

Part 7

Summary and Useful Information

21

Summary

Danny Blyth

Life isn't getting any easier for the modern independent publican. Once upon a time not so long ago most pubs were much of a muchness in what they had to offer as they each tried to appeal to as wide a section of the community as they could. Competition for the leisure pound in those times when leisure was a rare word for many and a perk of but a few wasn't nearly as strong. How times change.

Today's pub has to compete hard for food and drink sales with everything from the bar at the local leisure centre to the new café that's appeared in the local church's crypt (many of whom have also become licensed).

There are big brands to deal with, pub chains with a claim on the young, others with beer so cheap they're selling at a price not far off what you might be buying in at.

Publicans have always had to be people of many parts – friend, social worker, psychologist, host and provider of victuals. However, nowadays they also have to be modern retailers with as much know-how concerning cappuccino as G&T. They must also be caterers able to compete with any other – marketeers, promoters and merchandisers and motivational leaders to manage staff now judged against anywhere else by today's more demanding customer spends.

The challenge is tough already. And it isn't getting any easier. But the successful independent pub isn't dying; far from it. Look at the way any successful free house is bought out quickly after a decision to sell has been made. Notice also how the amount of initiatives taken by enterprising independent traders have been transformed into concepts and rolled out across the nation.

What has happened is that pubs have improved. Publicans are appreciating much more how, if they are to succeed, it is the sum of various parts of this new modern business that have to combine to make for a great experience for the customer. After all, there are more excuses today than ever before for any one person to sway a group away from visiting a particular pub: 'There's no vegetarian food there,' 'Kids aren't particularly welcome,' 'Their coffee is always weak,' 'It's only got two types of Breezer' etc.

Just having a good pint now seems laughable, and yes, it really was once enough to get you by. Today though, the pub has at least to try and be much better at a wide range of things to suit a wider range of customer. There are increasing calls for pubs to be places to eat or taste wines, to act as pre-club venues or somewhere for the family to go for a treat. The publican himself has to be computer literate, an operator cum 'mover and shaker' as much as a host. High standards are demanded and expected in many new areas.

And it is in trying to suggest new approaches to these fresh challenges that we have brought in a new look *Publican's Handbook*. We trust it has been of use and welcome your feedback.

We are confident the trade will prosper, continuing to develop in accordance with what people want. This ability to adapt is one tradition of the trade that is as strong as ever.

Useful Addresses and Phone Numbers

Academy of Food and Wine Service
Burgoyne House
Burgoyne Quay
8 Lower Teddington Road
Hampton Wick
Surrey KT1 4ER
Tel: 020 8943 1011
Fax: 020 8977 5519

Advisory, Conciliation, and Arbitration Service (ACAS)
Brandon House
180 Borough High Street
London SE1 1LW
Tel: 020 7210 3000

AIR (for more information on the Public Places Charter)
1–5 Poland Street
London W1F 8PR
Tel: 020 7482 0620
Fax: 020 7482 0620
Web: www.airinitiative.com
Email: enquiries@airinitiative.com

Alliance of Independent Retailers
Alliance House
Bank Chambers
5–9 St Nicolas Street
Worcester WR1 1UW
Tel: 01905 612733
Fax: 01905 21501

Association of Licensed Free Traders
Dane House
55 London Road
St Albans
Herts AL1 1LJ
Tel: 01727 841644
Fax: 01727 852208

Association of Licensed Multiple Retailers
3rd Floor
International House
Ealing
London W5 5DB
Tel: 020 8579 2080
Fax: 020 8840 6217

Association of Valuers of Licensed Property
c/o 18 Bloomsbury Square
London WC1A 2NS
Tel: 020 7636 8992

Brewers and Licensed Retailers Association
42 Portman Square
London W1H 0BB
Tel: 020 7486 4831
Fax: 020 7935 3991

British Hospitality Association
Queens House
55–56 Lincoln's Inn Fields
London WC2A 3BH
Tel: 020 7404 7744
Fax: 020 7404 7799

British Entertainments & Disco Association
5 Waterloo Place
Stockport
Cheshire SK1 3AZ
Tel: 0161 429 0012

British Institute of Innkeeping
Wessex House
80 Park Street
Camberley
Surrey GU15 3PT
Tel: 01276 684449
Fax: 01276 23045
Web: www.bii.org
Email: info@bii.org

British Meat Federation
12 Cock Lane
London EC1A 9BU
Tel: 020 7329 0776

British Safety Council
70 Chancellors Road
London W6 9RS
Tel: 020 8741 1231

Campaign for Real Ale (CAMRA)
230 Hatfield Road
St Albans
Herts AL1 4LW
Tel: 01727 867201
Fax: 01727 867670

Cask Marque
Seebed Centre
Severalls Park
Colchester
Essex C04 4HT
Tel: 01206 752212
Fax: 01206 751198
Web: www.cask-marque.co.uk
Email: cask-marque@mcno.com

Catering Equipment Suppliers Association
Carlyle House
235–237 Vauxhall Bridge Road
London SW1V 1EJ
Tel: 020 7233 7724
Fax: 020 7828 0667

CEDA
Catering Equipment Distributors Association
PO Box 194
Bingley
West Yorks BD16 2XW
Tel: 01274 826056
Fax: 01274 777260
Email: secretary@ceda.co.uk

CESA
Catering Equipment Supplies Association
Carlyle House
235–237 Vauxhall Bridge Road
London SW1V 1EL
Tel: 020 7233 7724
Fax: 020 7828 0667
Web: www.cesa.org.uk

Chartered Institute of Environmental Health
Chadwick Court
15 Hatfields
London SE1 8DJ
Tel: 020 7928 6006
Fax: 020 7827 5865

City and Guilds
1 Giltspur Street
London EC1A 9DD
Tel: 020 7294 2468
Fax: 020 7294 2400

Cleaning & Hygiene Suppliers Association
PO Box 770
Marlow
Bucks SL7 2SH
Tel: 01628 478273

Confederation of Tourism, Hotel and Catering Management
118–120 Great Titchfield Street
London W1P 7AJ
Tel/Fax: 020 7612 0170

Cookery and Food Association
1 Victoria Parade
331 Sandycombe Road
Richmond
Surrey TW9 3NB
Tel: 020 8948 3870
Fax: 020 8332 6326

Dept of Employment
Sanctuary Buildings
Great Smith Street
London SW1P 3BT
Tel: 020 7925 5000

Employment Rights Advice Service
27–29 Amwell Street
London EC1R 1TL
Tel: 020 7713 7583

English Tourism Council
Thames Tower
Blacks Road
London W6 9EL
Tel: 020 8563 3000
Fax: 020 8563 0302

English Wine Society
Vine House
Glade Road
Marlow
Bucks SL7 1DZ
Tel: 01628 482299

Federation of Licensed Victuallers' Associations
126 Bradford Road
Brighouse
West Yorks HD6 4AU
Tel: 01484 710534
Fax: 01484 718647

Federation of Retail Licensed Trade
91 University Street
Belfast BT7 1HP
Tel/Fax: 028 9032 7578

Food From Britain
123 Buckingham Palace Road
London SW1W 9SA
Tel: 020 7233 5111

Guild of Master Victuallers
Royal Six Bells
222 High Street
Colliers Wood
London SW19 2BH
Tel: 020 7222 5300

Health and Safety Executive
Information Services
Broad Lane
Sheffield
South Yorks S3 7HQ
Tel: 0541 545500
Fax: 0114 289 2333

HM Customs & Excise
Dorset House
Stamford Street
London SE1 9PY
Tel: 020 7928 3344

The Hospitality Training Foundation
International House
3rd Floor
High Street
Ealing
London W5 5DB
Tel: 020 8579 2400
Fax: 020 8840 6217

HSE Books
PO Box 1999
Sudbury
Suffolk CO10 2WA
Tel: 01787 881165

Licensed Retail Consultants
(Paul Cooper)
46 Front Street
Slip End
Luton
Bedfordshire
Tel: 01582 424484

Licensed Trade Charities Trust
The Brows, Sutton Place
Abinger Hammer
Dorking
Surrey RH5 6RL
Tel: 01306 731223

Licensed Victuallers' Trade
Association (London & South-east)
The Royal Six Bells
222 High Street
Colliers Wood
London SW19 2BH
Tel: 020 8540 1275
Fax: 020 8540 2715

Licensed Victuallers' Trade
Association (Midlands)
Larkfield
Ashlawn Road
Rugby CV22 5QE
Tel: 01788 553353
Fax: 01788 535626

Licensed Victuallers' Trade
Association (West)
The Benett Arms
Semley Nr Shaftesbury
Dorset SP7 9AS
Tel: 01747 830221
Fax: 01747 830152

Licensed Victuallers Wales
2 Derwendeg Station Road
Govilon
Abergavenny
Gwent NP7 9RG
Tel/Fax: 01873 830415

London Tourist Board
Glen House, Stag Place
London SW1E 5LT
Tel: 020 7932 2000

Music Alliance
29–33 Berners Street
London W1P 4AA
Tel: 020 7580 5544
Fax: 020 7306 4050

National Pubwatch
17 Chace Avenue
Potters Bar
Hertfordshire
EN6 5LX
Tel: 01707 650095
Email: m.eidmans@btinternet.com

Office of Fair Trading
Field House
15–25 Breams Buildings
London EC4A 1PR
Tel: 020 7211 8000

Pannone & Partners
123 Deansgate
Manchester M3 2BU
Tel: 0161 909 3000
Fax: 0161 909 4444

Performing Rights Society
29/33 Berners Street
London W1P 4AA
Tel: 020 7580 5544

Portman Group
7–10 Chandos Street
London W1G 9DQ
Tel: 020 7907 3700
Fax: 020 7907 3710
Web: www.portman-group.org.uk
Email: info@portmangroup.org.uk

Restaurant Association
Africa House
64–78 Kingsway
London WC2B
Tel: 020 7831 8727

Royal Society for the Prevention of Accidents (RoSPA)
Edgbaston Park
353 Bristol Road
Birmingham B5 7ST
Tel: 0121 248 2000
Fax: 0121 248 2001

Scottish Licensed Trade Association
10 Walker Street
Edinburgh EH3 7LA
Tel: 0131 225 5169
Fax: 0131 220 4057

Scottish Tourist Board
23 Ravelston Terrace
Edinburgh EH4 3TP
Tel: 0131 332 2433
Fax: 0131 343 1513

Society of Licensed Victuallers
Heatherley
London Road
Ascot SL5 8DR
Tel: 01344 844440

Sussex Society of Licensed Victuallers
Pearn House, 98 Riley Road
Brighton
East Sussex BN2 2AH
Tel: 01273 682743

The Tourism Society
26 Chapter Street
London SW1P 4ND
Tel: 020 7834 0461

The Vegetarian Society
Parkdale, Dunham Road
Altrincham
Cheshire
WA14 4QG
Tel: 0161 925 2000

Wales Tourist Board
Brunel House
2 Fitzalan Road
Cardiff CF24 0UY
Tel: 029 2049 9909
Fax: 029 2048 5031

Wine & Spirit Education Trust
Five Kings House
1 Queen Street Place
London EC4R 1QS
Tel: 020 7236 3551
Fax: 020 7329 8712

Index of Advertisers